Smart A.S.S. for Your B.S.

Jody N Holland

ISBN:1-63390-055-X
ISBN-13: 978-1-63390-055-4

DEDICATION

I love sarcasm, wit, and the chance to fully express myself. I have been encouraged by several smart Awesome Stupendous Someones out there. You know who you are, and I thank you for your commitment to being fully you!

Table of Contents

Author's Note and Acknowledgement

I acknowledge that writing is difficult and sometimes it pushes me to live fully into who I am. I wrote this book because I needed to remind myself of whom I was supposed to be, how I was supposed to live, and that following the right model sometimes sucks ass, but it does bring incredible results. Life is not always easy even when the answer may be directly in front of us. Success requires sacrifice as well as dedication and sometimes the risk of being rejected by people who may very well judge you for not being just like them. I realize that I am not always going to be liked by others. At some point, you have to step out of the shadows and claim your place in this world, the one you have always known was yours. I am stepping out of the shadows. I acknowledge you for being on the journey. I recognize the challenges of life and the opportunities of life as well. Let's kick some ass together!

1 B.S.[3] – Business Strategy (b.S.), Belief Systems (B.s.), and BullShit (B.S.)

"However beautiful the strategy, you should occasionally look at the results."
– Sir Winston Churchill

Prelude To Conquering Life Together

This book is organized to walk you through the journey of success in the fastest way possible. A Smart A.S.S. (Accelerated Success System) is meant to collapse time for you, the reader. To accelerate success is to learn to think through your journey in such a way that you are propelled forward, crushing your limits and opening up your possibilities. As you go through this book and go on this journey, you will have to face the challenges of your limiting beliefs. You will stare self-doubt in the face, kick self-criticism in the gut, and body slam the use of the wrong strategies. These internal things you are facing are the only things holding you back. When you get them right, all the world collaborates for your success. You will begin by learning about your belief systems, how they impact your business strategies, and what bullshit you need to eliminate. You will use that knowledge to grasp hold of what actually is 'about you' and what actions you can take to be in control of yourself. Next, you will step into the arena of success and learn to fight for who the successful version of you is. This fight will require you to use your fundamental understanding of truth, of self, and of the world around you to shift the tides of success to your favor. Once you have turned the tides, you will need to up your leadership mentality. The first and most important person each of us will lead is ourselves. Once you begin to lead on purpose, you must find the strength to lead with purpose. Having a transcendent purpose will always take you past just the pursuit of money. When you are on the right path, money will always pursue you. For those who are building an organization, a downline, or a following, your ability to create culture will determine the tribe that is behind you. Having a following, you are able to write the future into existence that is right for you. With a clear vision of your future in hand, you will build your momentum of success by becoming a goal-digger, being relentless in living into your purpose and leading yourself and others on purpose. The temptation for many is to give everything they have up front, but we are in a marathon, not a sprint. By learning to get rid of the things that distract you from your purpose, you both maintain balance in life and maintain solid direction. By this point, if you are applying what you are learning, you will have direction, momentum, and drive. The key to succeeding at your highest level is to stay buzzed with the right energy of success. This step, as well as the rest of the steps, will require you to own your shit.

More than once, you will read about meditation in this book. Why meditation, you ask? Well, meditation has been scientifically proven to rewire the neuropathways of the brain to promote calm, clear thinking, even in stressful situations. My objective for you is to accelerate your ability to succeed. You must learn to keep yourself in the right state to stay focused on moving forward. Your state is the overall feeling you have about you at any given moment in time. With the right state, you are better equipped to create a story for yourself that supports your drive, desires, and vision of the future. It is our story that ultimately determines whether or not we are willing to implement the right strategy or strategies for winning. If your story is that you are not good at talking to other people, then you will not reach out as required to share your product, service, or opportunity. If your story is that you believe in a product or service so much that you would never keep others from experiencing its greatness, then you share the product or service proudly and continuously. If you implement what is outlined in the chapters of this book, you will see rapid and positive changes in yourself and therefore your success endeavors. My desire is for anyone who reads these pages to live a better life, a more abundant life, a life that has filled your positive dreams. Let's go kick some ass together!

Lift your foot! It's time to kick some ass!

We are who we are and where we are because we have chosen to be here. This thought haunted me as I started my journey to finding success. How could I have chosen to be in struggle? That didn't make any sense to me. I had friends who were struggling in business as well, and I really didn't think they had chosen that path either. It seemed to be an incredibly strange thought to have, particularly when I knew that I wanted my life to be better, easier, more filled with fun and adventure. The truth, however, was what began to unlock the layers and layers of conditioning that I had adopted, and, in the end, it was the truth that set me free.

The tough challenge that we face is that we have been sold a load of BS (bullshit) when it comes to finding success. We are supposed to hustle, and grind, and then rise and grind, and then work harder than everyone around us, and then… and then what? My first four years in business, I did not take any vacation. My first year, I did not take a single day off. That's right, I worked 365 days in a row. In year four, I began to realize that my dream of being an entrepreneur and having more freedom was, well, a load of BS. My Bs (belief system) was wrong and therefore, my bS (business strategy) was to work myself to death without achieving the right results. That seemed like a load of BS (bullshit) to me. I set a goal to take four weeks off in my fifth year of business. I had to master the Bs that it would work and create a better bS in order to make it work, so that I got out of the BS of a life that wasn't what I actually wanted.

I would like to tell you that the moment you master the first change, everything in your world will work perfectly for the rest of your life, but that would probably be BS for you, just like it was for me. The truth is that you will continuously build your Bs (belief system) to support your connection to the energy around you. You will invest in yourself from this point forward in order to find your path to true success and freedom. Your Belief system will ultimately influence your business Strategy and lead you to a better version of life. This is how you get rid of the bad Bull Shit in your life that is holding you back. You have to be willing to face each of the bs's though, in order to move your life forward and achieve your desired outcomes. Are you willing? Are you ready? We'll see!

Strategic Deception

We spend a great deal of time deceiving ourselves when it comes to finding success. We look to quick fixes and want others to do things for us when the truth is that we are each responsible for our place in life. You are who you are and where you are because you have made a series of choices that got you there and made you… you. I am not saying the circumstances of life don't influence the place where you end up. Instead, I am saying that regardless of the influence, having a real strategy enables you to keep your eyes on the prize. At some point in your childhood, you decided that you were either going to finish high school or not. You decided to either go to college or not. You decided to either work hard in your job or not. You made those decisions. The hard truth is that nobody is to blame for where you are right now. The deception lies in the victimhood of a person's viewpoint. You cannot be a victim and still find your victory. Victimhood puts you in a place of thinking that your strategy can't work when it has been proven to work for others. If another person has been able to accomplish what you wish to accomplish, then it is possible for you as well.

Napoleon Hill was born into poverty in Virginia in 1883. His mother passed when he was 10, and his father was busy trying to provide and had little time for discipline. Two years after his mother passed, his father remarried. By the time he remarried, Napoleon had already become a rebellious young man and had the habit of carrying a pistol with him wherever he went. In several of his speeches, he recounts how the influence of his stepmother changed the course of his life. She bought him a typewriter and taught him to channel his imagination and energy into writing. By the age of 13, he was a mountain reporter for a local paper. He could have stayed with the anger of losing his mother and not having the presence of his father much in his life. Or, he could have listened to his stepmother and charted a new course. Even at the age of 13, we have the capacity for making choices. Not only did Napoleon clean up his act, his father did as well. Hill began to see how surrounding yourself with people who have a vision for success can change everything. Even further, he found that having a definite purpose in life changes your strategic direction as well as the energy with which you run your life. People do influence us, but each of us is responsible for our own decisions in the end.

It is often much easier to lie to ourselves and say that we are not at fault for the things going on in our lives. It is, however, still a lie. Strategic deception looks for any way that it can to pull us away from our potential and keep us in mediocrity. When a person is using this kind of thinking, they believe that life is happening to them. They believe that other people, the circumstances, the trials of life are what make them into who they are. What do you believe about yourself? Do you believe that life is happening to you? Do you believe that you have no control over what happens next? If so, you are practicing strategic deception in your life and you are moving away from your potential instead of towards it.

There is a reason why you see the world the way that you do. You see the world as you have made it, not as it really is. James Allen once said, "To think what one wants to think is to think the truth." Wow! Does this mean that there really isn't an absolute truth? Yes, it does. It means that each person creates their version of the truth through the labels that they create in life. It means that even if you grow up in the same house as your siblings, with the same parents, go to the same school, even with the exact same teachers, you will still create your own version of the truth of your existence. It isn't the experience that matters. It is the process of inception and assimilation that creates you as you are today.

The Process of Inception

"The outer conditions of a person's life will always be found to be harmoniously related to his inner state... Men do not attract that which they want, but that which they are."
--James Allen, from As a Man Thinketh.

Why do you view the world like you do right now? What process did you follow to create your current view of reality, of this world? How were your beliefs and interpretations of reality constructed? Those are questions that each of us must answer on our journey. Both our chosen interpretation of reality and our explanation of why will determine our destination. We will either accelerate toward success or accelerate toward failure based on who we are from the inside out. Your worldview is an intricate tapestry of experiences labeled with meaning and then used to filter the next and the next and the next experience. When you were born, you did not have any preconceived notions about what it meant to be successful or to be a failure. You simply lived life for survival. Babies are born with only two fears. They fear falling and loud noises. That's it. They are not afraid of public speaking, social embarrassment, or the potential that the cute girl/guy in 7th grade won't like them. They don't fear anything else. They also don't need the approval of others. At 2:37 AM, when they soil themselves while sleeping, they don't think about whether or not their screaming will impact their parents or siblings. They simply scream until they are taken care of properly. Life happens as the child, not to the child. During this initial development phase, the brain waves function as if the infant is in a hypnotic state. They are slow and long, allowing for quick adaptation of motor skills, language development, and core personality development. Each infant is a mix of the genetic markers passed on from their biological parents and the nurturing that they are exposed to or lacking during this time. This core development goes on for the first 6 years of a child's life, with a shift beginning around 4 to 4 ½ years old, depending on the young person. The shift is that from being imprinted with the ideas of the world around them to being able to consciously process and make choices from the world within them.

By the age of 7, the core personality as well as the core understanding of right and wrong are developed in the average human. During this phase of development, we **act**. We act according to a delicate blend of genetics and inputs. Now comes the influence of potential and pattern overlays. From the age of 7 through the age of 13, a young person seeks out models for their world. They look for the values and characteristics that seem to feel right and at the same time, make sense cognitively. They may latch on to real people, such as parents or coaches or teachers, or they may latch on to characteristics of fictional characters, such as super-heroes, or the persona of a superstar athlete or musician. They begin to seek out ways to construct themselves from little bits of other people. This process is at a high point around the age of 10, as they absorb the values and beliefs of those people who make the most sense to them. Having a child spend time around positive role models is very important. I believe that we are the average of our five closest relationships. Unfortunately, these relationships can consist of gaming consoles and smart phones. During this stage of development, young people begin to give meaning to each of the experiences they have. They label the evaluation of others as either good or bad. They label the image of themselves as positive or negative. They then use these labels to assign meaning to future events. This process happens in a portion of the brain known as the Apperception Mass. This small portion of the brain is responsible for maintaining the labels and filters that we use to evaluate each new experience. When a person is teased for wearing a certain brand of clothing, they begin to associate both the social situation and the brand of clothing with the feeling of being teased. During this phase of development, we react.

We experience primary emotions as we go through this phase of life, and we begin to associate experiences with the emotion that was connected with it. The emotion itself doesn't move from one space to the next in the grid in our minds, but the experience can be removed from the emotional placeholder. Our emotions stay in the same place, but our experiences can move by removing the emotional label given to them.

Sadness	Versus	Joy
Anger	Versus	Fear
Surprise	Versus	Anticipation
Distrust	Versus	Trust

Each emotion has its opposite. When you think about the emotions you experience, you realize that the opposite of sadness is joy, or the opposite of surprise is anticipation, and so on. The following graphic will help you understand how to evaluate your emotional states to see what you are experiencing.

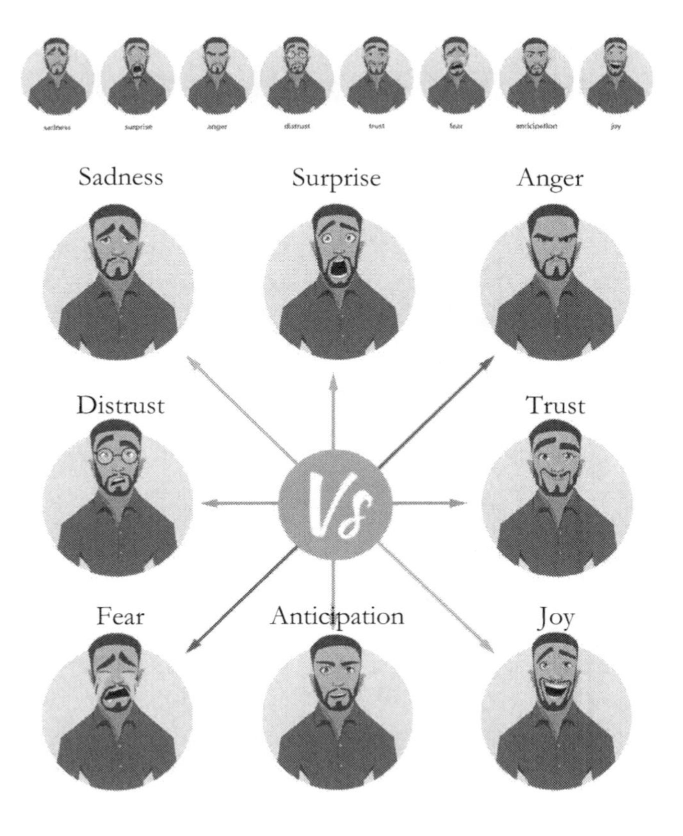

Our label maker of a mind strives to bring order to a world of seeming chaos. It seeks out ways to put things in a predictable order for the quickest possible recall and/or evaluation. Think back to the experiences you had as a youngster. There is a good chance that because of either pain or pleasure, you chose to model yourself after another person (pleasure) or the opposite of a person (pain). We pursue pleasurable experiences, and we avoid painful ones. It is the way the human brain is hardwired. As we find our models, we prepare to move into the third phase of becoming the person that we are today. We learn to connect.

This is where our process of connecting the dots from what was enacted upon us and what we acted upon converges. During this third phase of development, we seek ways to connect not only the dots of previous programming, but also to connect ourselves into a complex world of meaning. This process is accompanied with the release of large amounts of hormones into the bloodstream which can cloud the previous programming and prompt young people to test the limits of their labels. The anchor of values that were implanted by parents and teachers and coaches and other role models in a young person's life seek to keep them close to the replication of the lessons. Yet, the need for independence and additional connection as a result of hormonal floods in the brain prompt them to try out new models of thought and feeling. To connect with the world around us means to connect the self with the meaning given to the various aspects of the world. Which group of people best connects a person to who they feel and think that they truly are? Which activities and endeavors best represent the soul of the person? As a young person battles to become a grown person, they must learn key lessons. The challenge of controlling the meaning of events in one's own mind remains with them for their entire lives. The lesson is a filtered experience based on previous meanings / labels given to experiences that were similar in nature. Each experience builds off of the previous and adds to or takes away the meaning already there. By the time a person reaches between 22 (females) and 26 (males), their capacity for thinking critically about the meaning of life in a given experience is developed. This aspect of thought continues to develop throughout one's life, but the cloud of hormonal interference slows, and life begins to be more understandable.

During this third phase of development, skills such as critical thinking, problem-solving, self-accountability, and decision-making are developed. If a young person is not held accountable for making their choices, then these skills struggle to develop for much of their life. In this third phase, one's mind battles to understand how to create meaning and move out of the belief that life is happening to them. If they are not prepared by parents, teachers, and others to have radical responsibility for self, the lessons that could make life flow later are missed. I believe this is why Napoleon Hill stated that 98% of people are drifters, believing that life happens to them instead of by them. In Hill's book, Outwitting The Devil, Mr. Earthbound interrogates the devil to discover the pathway out of suffering (Hill, 2011). The devil is forced to confess the model to be followed but makes a point of explaining that this third phase of development is his playground. He often taps into the minds of teenagers and corrupts them to believe that they have no real control of themselves. What was your mind like as a teenager? Were you in control of self? Did your parents or guardians require you to be responsible? Did they blame you for what went wrong, praise you for what went right, or attempt to control your very thoughts? To truly be free, one must learn to let go of the label of an experience and embrace the truth that any label that is desired today can be applied to any experience past or present.

If you find that the labels created for your life and through your experiences do not serve you, then it is time for a change. It is time to be honest with yourself and claim the power that has always been yours. You are the creator of your reality whether that be good or bad. You are the only one who can change what an experience of yours has meant. Will you claim that power, or will you lie to yourself and say that the world, or a teacher, or a parent, or a circumstance is to blame for your inability to move forward? It is time to step up and confront the truth! It is time for you to be the best you possible.

I Have To Be Honest

An honest strategy is one that actually works, regardless of what your instincts are telling you. Often times, your instincts are shitty little liars. They tell you that you would be better off waiting on someone else or some other business model to fix you. My wife and I joke about my instincts when driving. For some reason, she got built-in, brain-powered GPS, and I did not. When it seems like I should go right, it is probably to the left. She can be in almost any country in the world and have a feel for the right direction to go in order to get to the proper destination. On the other hand, I have a fairly strong instinct for knowing what will work to take a client in the right direction to find success. The challenge that each of us faces is knowing when our instincts are right and when they are wrong. After all, the objective is to move in the right direction to find success for ourselves and our businesses.

Building your criteria for measured success is the first step in understanding whether or not your strategy is working. I recall a story that I have heard several speakers use over the years, including my father. It goes something like this…

> *I was coming home late one evening and was pretty tired. As I got out of my car at the house and headed toward the front door, I cut across the yard to save a little time. The lights were not on anyway, so I figured it was easier than going to the sidewalk. I had my keys in my hand, my backpack with my laptop, and two notebooks, as well as my used cup from coffee that morning. A few steps into the grass, I realized that I had dropped something. I made it to the house and reached for my keys only to realize that it was my keys I had dropped. I found the chair that sits by the front door and sat all of my stuff down in the chair. I tried to retrace my steps toward the car and remember the spot where I realized I had dropped something… my keys. I searched with my foot at first since it was really dark in that area and then eventually got down on my hands and knees to search for*

them. After a few minutes of searching, I noticed that at the edge of my yard, right where my neighbor's yard started, they had a light on a light pole. I headed toward the pole and began to search there because the light was so much better. My neighbor noticed me crawling around in his yard after a few minutes and came out to check on me. He asked me what I was doing, and I told him that I had dropped my keys in the yard and was having trouble finding them. He began to search with me, trying to find the keys so that I could get in my house. After 5 or so minutes of searching together, he asked me how I had dropped my keys in the edge of his yard when I was parked in my own driveway. I looked up and told him that I hadn't. I dropped them close to my driveway, but the light was so much better here.

I was never going to find my keys in a place that I had not dropped them. I was only going to search in vain and even drag my neighbor into the futile search process as well. This is often what we do in life. We go to what we know before what we don't know because it is comfortable. We know how to search when everything is visible. We tend to do what is easy before what is hard. I see this in goal-setting as well. They start with something that is insignificant and then go to the next barely significant thing instead of doing the things that will have a lasting impact. Your strategy is your lie when it is not moving you toward your stated goal. Even if it is what you have been doing for years, it only matters if it is actually working. So, ask yourself a question right now… "Is what I am doing moving me toward my ultimate goal?" If the answer to the question is no, then it is time to be honest. You have chosen the easy path, where the light is shining, instead of the true path to your success. It is time for you to step up and make some changes in your strategy and in your beliefs if you actually want to win. The other question that you have to answer honestly is… "Do I actually want to be successful?" If the answer is yes, then you will have to do what is necessary to be successful. If the answer is no, which it seems to be for a massive amount of people in this world, then stop whining about not having what you desire, put this book down, and go back to failing on purpose in life. I struggle to believe that you would have even picked up a book on success unless, at your core, you desired to move your life forward. If you are like me, and you likely are, since you picked up a book titled Smart A.S.S. for your B.S., then keep moving forward. It is time to kick your A.S.S. into high gear and accept the truth that you have not done a proper evaluation of your strategy. It is time to step up and kick the lie to the curb, embrace the truth of what you need to do to be successful, and move forward with the strategy that does produce results for you.

You have to take the bull by the horns, so to speak, and fix yourself. Hope is not a strategy. It is an illusion of things changing without any evidence to back it up. When you take the bull by the horns, you are facing your problems head on. You are accepting that you have not made the right decisions and you're kind of pissed off about it. You are angry enough to no longer be willing to accept anything less than the best effort from yourself. Just like most people, I have things that I have hated about myself. I still have some lies that crop up from time to time and make me feel all comfortable yet lead me to failure. When I first went into business, I did not want to cold call people. I still hate cold calling. Thirty days into being in business in 1999, I realized that my two options were to give up the lie that people would track me down to do business with me even though I had never proven anything to anyone, or embrace the truth that I had to hustle and grind to build my own success. I had to kick my own ass every day to make myself pick up the phone and call people. As much as I dislike organizing my desk, it seemed like a great idea every time I got to call time. I kept looking for other things to do that would allow me to blame the world around me instead of accepting responsibility for myself and my results. In my first 30 days, I made 3 phone calls, 3 presentations, and sold $2,000 in training. I realized very quickly that 3 presentations per month and 1 or 2 small contracts per month were going to land me in the poor house. This was evident because $2,000 was about 33% of what I was making monthly in my job before I quit and started my business. I was the one who was being bull-headed and not wanting to put myself in the pain of possibly being rejected. When I finally grabbed my own bull-headed stubbornness by the horns and slammed the wussy to the ground, I became the entrepreneur that I was supposed to be.

Things began to work in my favor when I accepted full responsibility for myself. In my first 52 weeks of business, I made roughly 3600 cold calls, attended 24 networking events, presented to 500 potential clients, and sold right at $112,000 in training. That is significantly better than when I started. It was a choice to do what was needed versus a choice to be a wuss and blame other things.

I began to be proud of what I had to offer, and I gave up the lie of the world finding me because of my website or my imagined reputation. 19 years later, I still call on people, but I don't have to do the same number of cold calls as I did in the past. I have a reputation for helping clients. I have a reputation for bringing financial and personal success to people's lives, to their businesses, and ultimately to their families and communities. I now use this as my resource for success. I leverage my efforts and the reputation I have built to continue to thrive as an author, speaker, trainer, and coach.

Find the resources you need, but don't wait for the resources to show up magically. The resources that I needed in order to move myself forward in the beginning of my business came to me in the form of a business coach. 30 days into business I realized that I had no freaking clue what I was doing. My first business coach was named Mack, and he was the one who revealed my self-deception for what it was. He helped me outline a model of calling, presenting, and closing that would serve me for years to come. I did not know what I did not know. I needed the resource of a person who had already been there and done that so that I could find the success that I desired.

The Truth Is A Lie

The truth is dependent upon what you think. To think what one wishes to think is to think one's own version of truth. The truth isn't true, though. In fact, the truth doesn't exist. What is it that you can say that would always be true for everyone, everywhere? Keep thinking. You can't even say that religious beliefs are true for everyone everywhere. I am not picking a fight here. In fact, I simply want you to acknowledge how strongly you feel that what is true to you should be true to everyone, everywhere. When we really inspect what we believe to be the truth and then compare our truth to that of another person, it becomes evident that the only thing that is absolute is that there really are no absolutes.

We often get hung up on our beliefs because they seem so real to us. We allow the truth that we are not great salespeople, or public speakers, or that we can't stand up for ourselves to become the truths that rule our lives. Think about some of the things that you have believed to be true that have been holding you back from chasing your dreams, or fulfilling what you want your destiny to be. When you begin to look at your limiting belief systems, you realize that they are truly limiting B.S., and they aren't worth keeping. A few examples that I have either thought or heard from coaching clients are…

1. I have never been in business before, so I can't start a business.
2. Nobody in my family ever takes risks, so I wouldn't be able to be that successful risk taker.
3. I can't speak in front of other people.
4. I don't know how to sell.
5. I need to have a book before I can start teaching things to others.

6 I need to suffer for a few years and put in my time in order to be successful.
7 I fail at everything.
8 I need money before I can make money.
9 If I call people that I have never met, they might reject me.
10 If I try, I might fail, so I will just stay doing what I am doing.

Which of those wrong B.s. (belief system) statements do you recall thinking and/or saying? I would imagine that you have at least thought several of them when it comes to pursuing your opportunities in life. B.s. (belief system) statements keep us from the greatness that is possible. I wasn't born into money. I wasn't born a leader. I did not have a book deal until well after 5 years old, and sometimes people don't like me. Who gives a shit? My job does not center around needing to be liked. It centers around having something of great value to offer the world and then kicking the ass of the scared kid inside of me so that the man in there can move life forward. You are the sum total of your choices. Your choices are simply the result of how you have labeled the world around you as you experienced it. If you want to change, change your interpretation!

Your truth is only your truth because it is the web of interpretations that you have chosen to overlay into the fabric of your reality. Nothing is real until you give it meaning. As I sit in the coffee shop writing this, my laptop is sitting on a table. I know this because I was taught that the thing with the keys and the screen that allows my brain to be shared with others is called a laptop. If I had been taught that it was called a "brain-ifier", then I would have called it that. We speak truth about the things around us based on the labels that we were taught and ultimately adopted as our own. Nothing in this world has meaning except for that which we give it. I am a writer because I have chosen to see myself as such. Because of the label I have accepted, I act as a writer. I do what writers do. I write. If I had labeled myself as not being able to write, you would not be reading this sentence right now, at least not from me. You create meaning. You create truth. Choose wisely!

You Are Not Your Khakis

This was a line from Fight Club. I love it because it helps us remember that we are not our clothes, or our circumstances, or our house, or our car, or any of our possessions. Those are just things that you have surrounded yourself with to try and gain meaning. We find others who we believe have meaning in life and attempt to emulate them. We want others to say things like, "Jody, you look just like Brad Pitt; you must be so happy." Anyone that has met me knows that I do not look just like Brad Pitt. He has a ways to go to become more Jody-like. If I am only good enough when I am someone else, then I will never be good enough. I love the video of Jim Carrey at the Golden Globe Awards. In his speech, he is introduced as 2-time Golden Globe Award Winner Jim Carrey. He proceeds to say that he is 2-time Golden Globe Award Winner Jim Carrey, and when he goes to bed to get some well-deserved shut-eye, he does it as 2-time Golden Globe Award

Winner Jim Carrey. He says that he dreams of becoming 3-time Golden Globe Award Winner Jim Carrey, because then he will be enough. Sometimes comedians are able to capture the essence of the absurdity of needing awards and affirmations in order to believe that we are enough. The reality is, you are enough just like you are. That doesn't mean that you are giving up on becoming more or striving for greatness. It does, however, mean that whether you make a million or make a thousand, you are still you. If you derive your meaning and your worth from achieving something else, it will always be something more and different that you need to feel worthy. This is regardless of what level of achievement you attain. If you make a million, then you will need $2,000,000 to be happy. Once you get that, you will need $3,000,000. It is never enough when you derive your worth outside of yourself. Please say the following with me… "I don't give a shit what anyone thinks of me. I am enough!"

You are you, and that is all you have ever needed to be. To find the right strategy, you need to let go of the image of success and embrace the action of success. Too many people get caught up in needing to drive the right car or have the right house without considering what a difference it would make if they simply acted in the right direction every single day. You are not your possessions. You are your thoughts, feelings, and actions. When your thoughts and feelings are in alignment, then your actions will flow in the right direction of success. When you think one direction and feel a different direction, then your actions will be scattered. One critical strategy you must embrace is that of aligning yourself with a truth that supports you moving forward, creating success, and being the full expression of you. The truth is that you will only be happy when you live into the greatness already inside of you.

"If you intentionally become less than you are capable of being, then I warn you, you will be unhappy for the rest of your life."

--Abraham Maslow, Father of Motivational Theory

2 Dr. Phil Was Wrong

"The more tranquil a man becomes, the greater is his success, his influence, his power for good. Calmness of mind is one of the beautiful jewels of wisdom."
--James Allen

It Ain't About You... Yes It Is!

Dr. Phil became famous for looking at people whom he considered to be self-absorbed or inattentive to the world around them and saying, "It ain't about you." This catch phrase was meant to jolt a person into the reality that they are not the center of the universe, not the only person in the two-person relationship. His intent was good in that he wanted people to be focused on how to resolve the problem instead of being caught in the asshole bubble of self-centeredness. The problem is... It is about you. It is about mapping out who you are and who you wish to be. It is about being the best version of self that is possible. Even with the individuals that he was wailing on, it was ultimately about them and the decisions that they were making. The way I see it, you will have to step back from your daily life and begin to look at who you have chosen to be instead of looking for a way to rationalize your lack of responsibility for your choice. Next, you will have to accept the reality that you are here to create yourself, not to find yourself. If you feel that you need to find yourself, just look in a mirror and voila, there you are. Life is about creation. You were born to be a creator… so begin with your greatest masterpiece. Create you!

The roadmap to creating a better version of yourself begins with understanding where you are right now. Think about it. When you choose a destination on your navigation app or the car's GPS, it always begins with you being identified at a specific point on the map. In life, you have to be realistic about and truly know your starting point. This means tuning in to what you actually believe about yourself and about your relationship to the world around you. Your beliefs will create the patterns of thought that you experience. Your thoughts always become things. It isn't that I can think hard about a Ferrari and end up with one in front of me that I own without any action. It doesn't mean that I can't get that either, if I accept that I am the type of person who works to realize my dream of being a Ferrari driver. However, when I believe that I am a Ferrari driver and I fully accept it and feel the Ferrari-ness at a cellular level, then my thoughts go to a place that explains to my body and the world around me what a

Ferrari driver thinks and ultimately does. Your thoughts guide you into the specific action plans you take. Those actions must be in alignment with your beliefs and thoughts. We experience cognitive dissonance when our thoughts and beliefs don't line up with our actions. It doesn't take long for us to go in a new direction when that happens. We ALWAYS end up acting in accordance with our beliefs and thoughts. This is how we generate results. If we reject or dislike the results we have achieved, then we are forced to believe something new which changes the trajectory of our belief loop and moves us to achieve different results. Examine the beliefs that you have about you without filtering the statements. The truth is the only thing that can set you free from the past B.s. (belief system) constraints.

Exercise Time

Take a few minutes and simply fill out the following five statements. Don't think about it… just fill out the first thing that comes to mind at the end of each statement. Each statement should be different than the one before. Ready? Go!

I am

I am

I am

I am

I am

Now for the tricky part; fill out the same five statements but do so as if you are living your perfect life. Everything is going exactly as it should go. Clients are coming out of the woodworks to do business with you. Your family is healthy and happy and loves you very much. Your coworkers, bosses, employees, friends, and everyone you meet thinks you are incredible. Take a moment and feel what it feels like for the world to be perfect. Hold onto the emotion and absorb the reality of perfection that you are holding in your mind. Kill the damn monkey in your brain trying to distract you! Now, feel it and see it and accept it. Ready? Go!

I am

I am

I am

I am

I am

This is your brain

The emotional brain has been traditionally isolated in the hippocampus, amygdala, and the hypothalamus. These three components of the brain are responsible for the neurochemical production that leads to happiness, sadness, fear, anger, joy, surprise and anticipation. The traditional emotional responses are based on the beliefs that a person holds about their interaction with the world around them. For example, if you believe it is wrong to treat another human in an unkind way and then you witness an interaction that you label as unkind, you will feel an emotional response from that experience. When you anticipate something incredible is about to happen, you have the same euphoric high that you would when the incredible thing actually happens. The brain doesn't distinguish clearly between what is happening to you, what is about to happen to you, and what is happening to someone else. Your beliefs are filtered by another component of the brain known as the reticular activating system, or the RAS.

At a subconscious level, your brain has been programmed to look for specific things and then to reference the labels you have placed in the apperception mass in order to utilize the reticular activating system to filter what moves to conscious awareness. This is all happening beneath the surface for you, so it is a seamless and almost instantaneous process. You don't think about the meaning you have adopted. You simply feel. The prefrontal cortex houses your logical function and is a part of the conscious mind. The conscious mind has the power to send suggested belief changes to the subconscious, but it must be intentional. There are three times the brain is most open to transfer from conscious to subconscious. These times are when one first wakes in the morning, when one is drifting off to sleep, and when one's brain waves are in a hypnotic pattern. The hypnotic pattern of brain function can be achieved in a sleep-like state, which is achieved in meditation, prayer, hypnosis, and in the moments before one drifts off to sleep as well as shortly after one wakes.

Your mind is continuously being influenced. The question is whether it is being positively or negatively influenced. The fastest pathway to generating the right neurochemical rush for a positive feeling is to position your body to feel grateful, inspired, hopeful, and empowered. When you first wake, walk through a list of things that you are grateful for. List as many things as you can in your mind, or in a journal, or out loud. I love the aspect of journaling because it engages your mind, body, and visual processing. As you go through your list of things that you are grateful for, stay focused on generating a positive feeling about each of the things. Love into them. Love your spouse as you are grateful for them. Love your opportunities as you give thanks for them. Love your enemies as you are grateful for the strength they give you. Love yourself as you feel the greatness you have to offer the world around you. Really focus on the feeling you have when you love everyone and everything around you. Focus on how it feels to be grateful for every aspect of your life. When you believe that you are lucky and blessed, you are lucky and blessed. This whole process in the morning generally takes me less than 10 minutes.

At some point in the day, you need to take 5 to 10 minutes to meditate. During this meditation, hold an image in your mind of what life is like when it is easy, perfect, and everything has already gone your way. It is important to think of your life in the present tense as being amazing. Feel what it feels like for everything to be in your favor. Feel what it feels like for others to go out of their way to do business with you. Feel what it feels like for the entire universe to conspire for your success. Feel what it feels like for all of your relationships to be simple, easy, and in a positive flow state. Let go of any drama. Give up any worry about the future. Feel perfection in all of your interactions with the world around you. Hold the image and the feeling for 5 to 10 minutes during the day. If you are feeling down, simply close your eyes, position your body like you would if you had already won everything you could ever want in life, and feel into it for 1 minute. These short bursts of refueling coupled with intentional thought will continue to reshape your belief matrix, modifying the labels in your apperception mass and reprogramming your reticular activating system. This results in a significantly different response pattern from the hippocampus, hypothalamus, and amygdala.

Finally, as you drift off to sleep, list out at least 3 wins for the day and then feel into the image of success, love, joy, peace, and passion. Generate an image in your mind of everything being exactly as it should in each aspect of your world. Your finances are great. Your relationships are smooth and fulfilling. Your clients love you and pay promptly any time you invoice them. Your friends are supportive and build you up. Your life is amazing! See this reality. Feel this reality. Live this reality as you drift off to sleep. When you are intentional about what is in your mind before you fall asleep, you will find that your mind is positively influenced to relax more, rebuild your body and soul, and rekindle positive emotional responses. Sleeping is the reset of our cached memory. Like a computer, when you sleep, it wipes out what was in immediate memory and performs a reset for faster operation the next day. It is important not to plant a virus in your reset. Do not go to bed mad, holding an image of the world being out to get you. If you choose to push that virus into your operating system, it has devastating results on how you interpret the world around you. Reset things to perfect before drifting off to sleep. It may take a few nights of reset to get the bad programming out of your system. Trust me, the effort is absolutely worth it!

MF: or Magnetic Fields

Magnetic Fields are a fascinating concept when it comes to human interaction with the field. Dawson Church, in his book Mind To Matter, says that the magnetic field of a human can be measured at up to 15 feet away from the person in all directions. Every person you come within 15 feet of can be felt at a biological level. When you think about the projection of magnetic energy, you can compare it to that of simple magnets. When a metal is magnetized, it is because there are unpaired electrons within the metal itself. Since all matter is made up of atoms and atoms are made of protons, neutrons, and electrons, this would mean that all objects have the same fundamental structure. I get that I am not actually the man of steel, but steel and I are made up of atoms, which at least makes us cousins… I think. This unpaired electron, along with the other unpaired electrons, begin to spin together, which creates the polarity and magnetism.

What is fascinating about that explanation, at least to me, is that it is the stripping out of the negative and having it spin in a new direction. We are doing the same thing with our magnetic fields. When we build our Smart A.S.S. (Accelerated Success System) the right way, we strip away the negative energy and concentrate our positive energy with that of source energy, which has no polarity, in order to create a targeted direction for our life. I remember creating magnets as a kid for a science experiment. The process was not difficult but it did require a specific tactic. Moving a magnet along a piece of steel in the same direction over and over again changed the direction of the negative energy and began attracting through a magnetic pull.

Your mind operates in the same fashion. It will take more than one pass through of positive thought to generate a new spin to the negative thoughts that have been floating around. After all, there is a very good chance that you have been spinning negativity to repel good things for quite some time. If you believe, for example, that the world is out to get you or that every time you get close to success someone or something is going to pull the rug out from under you, then you will think about those things any time you get close to succeeding. This magnetic pull back into your comfort zone of being stuck and feeling that life sucks, or that others want ill for you, will draw you back into that experience. I know, I know. You are thinking, who the hell does this author guy think he is telling me that I am doing this to myself. Screw you author guy! Well, I think and believe that I am someone who has had the same experience and who was pissed off and offended to my core the first time someone told me that I am who I am and where I am because I have chosen to be there. Why the hell would I choose to not have the money and happiness that I said I wanted. The answer was simple. I was still the guy who was stuck, broke, unhappy, and unfulfilled… wanting to be the guy that was in flow, rich, happy, and fulfilled. We as humans only become that which we already are and never that which we wish to be. A little confused? Well, that means you have to see yourself at the next level, feel yourself at the next level, and act as if you are at the next level in order to generate the magnetic pull required for the next level to be in your life.

I have not traditionally been a big fan of feelings. People get them hurt too easily, and they stop themselves from being the full version of themselves because of what others might feel if they do. Having said that, I have come to discover the truth behind feelings. Feelings are the engine that drive the vehicle of your success. Your thoughts are the fuel, but the fuel is pointless without anything to run it. You do what you do because it feels like the right thing to do. You date the person you date because they feel right to you. You seek out ways to generate good feelings and to avoid or eliminate bad feelings. If you have bad feelings, you avoid the ones that you label as worse feelings. This last part can get you in trouble if you aren't careful. You can end up staying stuck because you feel that trying and failing at something might be worse than simply reusing your lame ass excuses for why you have failed over and over again. Your ability to magnetize an image of you being successful is what changes the polarity of your field and puts that signal out into the universe that you are truly ready for the next level of success. In the end, it's all YOU!

So, greet this day and every day with a healthy dose of gratitude and happiness. Your mood is the portrayal of your feelings. Your physiology, or physical posture, is the creator of your neurochemical and ultimately your hormonal flood into your system that we commonly refer to as your mood. So, do you own your mind, or are you the victim of mind control? Are you responsible for yourself, or are you just "an insignificant spec within an indifferent universe?" (Special thanks to Dr. Strange, the movie character, for that line)

This is my house

I will only live a full and rich life if I own the house I am living in. My body is my house. I have to take care of my diet. Your energy within this existence is predicated on your ability to generate energy. I made a crazy observation recently. I will not put regular low-octane unleaded in my car. I go out of my way to find gasoline with no ethanol. I often pay around $1 per gallon more for gas because it is better for my car. I care about the engine and the energy that it is able to produce, so I put the good stuff in it. When I made this observation, I was craving a candy bar! I put good stuff in my car because I care about the life of my car. What?! That made me start thinking about what I was craving and how I needed to be intentional about craving the right things.

We crave the things that are habitual for us. As I am typing this, I am sitting on an airplane. I just spent a couple of hours in an airport and a portion of that time was devoted to finding food that was not going to shorten the engine life of my body. I drink a healthy shake in the morning with power greens and lots and lots of blueberries. I have made a concerted effort to eat less fried food and drink less of the stuff that provides empty and pointless calories. I go to the gym at least 4 times per week, and I work out with intensity and purpose for the time I am there. I have also learned to rest more, get 7 hours of sleep per night, and meditate daily. I may not have this diet thing down perfectly yet, but I have noticed that since I began being intentional about what I put into my body, my body began to crave the things that were a part of my new eating habit. When I want a snack, I now crave almonds or fruit. When I am thirsty, I crave water more than sodas.

Learn to listen to what your body is telling you. Try out a few different models for feeding the engine that will create or destroy your chances of success and then pick a path. I still eat some red meat. I am, after all, in Texas. I eat less than I used to though because I feel more energy with fish, chicken, vegetables, and fruits. I have cut out a lot of the breads because I noticed that I started having brain fog when I consumed breads. I don't have a gluten allergy. I simply didn't feel as sharp.

I would encourage you to check out materials on healthy eating and try to eat more organic foods. I realize that eating healthy is a bit more expensive, but dying young will cost you everything. I am responsible for what I put into my body. I am not blaming anyone or anything for who I am. I am the only one who can make choices for how I will eat. I choose to feed my body as well as I would feed my car. Hey, I'm worth it! Are you?

This is my temple

You will only find success if you first find peace. The search for inner peace is at the center of most religions, at least in theory. People go to church in order to feel better about themselves and to be reminded that other people mess up and are forgiven just like them. As far as I can tell, Catholics go to confession in order for their sins to be absolved by the priest, and they are able to let go of their guilt and regret. I'm not Catholic, so I am just going off of what I have read on this one. Buddhists seek the inner light. Christians seek Jesus. The Church of the Flying Spaghetti Monster seeks noodley forgiveness and on and on. That last one was started as a joke, but now has over 1 million people who indicate they are followers. Each religion has their model of finding peace, but each is similar in that their followers must believe certain things and act in certain ways in order to be forgiven. In "A Course In Miracles," the text indicates that forgiveness is an illusion because we are already whole. We are already in communion with the source and made up of that source energy known as God and therefore don't need to seek a way out of truth. Instead, we need to accept the truth that we are made up of the very substance that is God and choose to live in the truth of our divine connection.

When I meditate, I feel that energy running through me, vibrating at a cellular level, and connecting me to all of life. I am not sure that I follow the appropriate Sanskrit models or any real models for that matter. What I do know is that my meditation helps me to see who I really am in my most pure form. I see the potential that exists for me, and that is me. I know that I feel better about life when I take the time to connect to my Source. My process adjusts based on what I am feeling that day. When my mind is particularly distracted, I kill the monkey mind by using a countdown model. When I feel less distracted, I use a gratitude and proclamation model. I will describe both of these to you and put a few options out there for different models that might work for you. What I do know is that meditation rewires your brain. It changes the manner in which information flows through your mind. It even changes the speed in which information can flow through your mind. It fundamentally changes your ability to be you… in a very good way!

The Countdown Method

The countdown method of meditation involves taking five deep breaths in through your nose and then out through your mouth. Your objective with the slow, deep breathing is to oxygenate your mind and allow you brainwave patterns to begin transitioning to a hypnotic state. This allows you to quickly and effectively have a positive impact on your mind, body, and emotions.

After the breaths, you imagine yourself at the top of a large staircase, or in my case a spiral staircase. You begin by saying, “As I count down from 100 to 90, I will descend into my subconscious mind.” I then visualize myself going effortlessly down the staircase. At about 95 in my countdown, I pass through a pitch black section of the spiral staircase and then end up at a pool of water when I hit 90. I love water so the water makes sense for me.

I then say, "As I count down from 89 to 80, I will release any attachment to this world. I will simply be." I am somehow in the water the moment I start counting down from 89. The water is the perfect temperature, and I am floating peacefully there. I am able to let go of the world and my thoughts and I focus just on breathing slowly, deeply, and fully as I imagine nothingness surrounding me. I imagine complete emptiness as I float and count down from 89 to 80.

I then say to myself, "As I count down from 79 to 70, I accept that I can construct anything I wish in my world without any effort. I will now build my life and my world as I would have it." I count down from 79 to 70 and visualize everything I desire in my world being true and coming true without having to put forth any significant effort. It simply comes into existence as I imagine it being. I bask in the truth that effort is not required to create greatness, but rather acceptance of greatness is required.

I then proceed with, "As I count down from 69 to 60, I see everyone around me as desiring good for me. They are going out of their way to help me succeed in everything that I do." As I count down, I visualize people from all over the world talking about how great I am and finding ways to support me, help me, and bring success to me. This requires nothing on my part. It is what each person in the world desires to do.

I then shift to my connection to all by saying, "As I count down from 59 to 50, I see and feel and know my connection to all things because I am made up of the very energy that makes up all things. Therefore, I am connected to all." Counting down to 50, I focus on how it feels to be connected at a source level to all existence. I see parts of the world and feel things from all over the world that support this belief.

Next, "As I count down from 49 to 40, I feel the love and support of my family and friends on my journey. They truly desire only the best for me." I then focus on the feeling of knowing that I am completely loved and supported by anyone whom I call family or friend in my life.

My next focus is on creative connection. I say, "As I count down from 39 to 30, I connect deeply to the source of all creativity and plug into the creative expression that will flow through me. I am divinely connected to Infinite Intelligence and accept the creative expression that the world needs through me." I then count down and both see and feel that creative expression flowing into and through me to the rest of the world. I see that expression touching the lives of everyone around me and extending out into the world to make the world better.

As I get close to the end of the countdown, I say, "As I count down from 29 to 20, I am filled with gratitude and know that I am truly blessed." I focus on seeing all of the things I am grateful for and on feeling grateful for everything in my life. This feeling of gratitude intensifies the energetic buzz that I experience at a cellular level.

I then move back into the pool of creation and accept the things that I have proclaimed into existence. I say, "As I float in the pool of creation, I am washed with success and charged with the energetic and magnetic attraction to bring all that I desire into existence. As I count down from 19 to 10, I accept that I Am that which I perceive that I Am." I then fully embrace the affirmations and proclamations I have made and see and feel all of the incredible things in my vision being true already.

Finally, I move back into conscious awareness by saying, "As I count down from 9 to 0, I ascend the staircase back into reality, fully accepting all that I have created as true and already in existence." I then count backwards from 9 to 0 and see myself climbing effortlessly up the spiral staircase. I pass through the pitch black section which represents the division between subconscious and conscious awareness around 5 and feel into the positive energy that now exists. As I get to 1 and then 0, I open my eyes and I am back, fully rested, fully alert, and ready to accept all that I have created.

I use this model when I need to ensure that my mind doesn't wander too much. Having a consistent countdown model allows my mind to focus on the countdown instead of focusing on trying to clear the distractions out of the way. You are welcome to change anything you wish in the visualization. These are the things that are effective for me. The whole process takes me about 10 minutes and really gives me a fantastic reset to my mental energy. I would encourage you to try this model out for several weeks. It is ideal that you pick a certain time of day and try to stay consistent on the 10 minutes that you devote to the countdown meditation. It can be the escape and rejuvenation you need in order to be consistently focused and on-target for your day.

This is my fortress

You will only live a full and rich life if you are in shape. You must take care of your body. You must move it and exercise it and ensure that it stays flexible. Toward the end of life, we long for more life, not more money. We look back on the things we have done and the things we wish we had done and evaluate who we are at that moment. Living a healthy life keeps your capacity for experiencing life at its highest point. I have read in several different places that we spend 80% of what we will spend on medical care in the last 10 years of our life. After all, most people will spend whatever money is necessary in order to have more life.

Staying in shape isn't about hitting the weights for 3 hours a day or having to go participate in HIIT, high intensity interval training, every day of the week. It is about staying in motion. Some of the healthiest people I know work in their yard for several hours a day. Some go to the gym for 15 minutes a day. It varies based on the person's body and their response to physical stimuli. What is it that you could do on a daily basis that would keep you in motion? What do you need to cut out to ensure that you stay in motion and don't sit around doing nothing?

For me, limiting the amount of time I spend watching TV or Netflix while sitting around has become critically important. When the series Breaking Bad came out on Netflix, I decided that I could only watch episodes while walking on the treadmill. I was so into the show that I would sometimes watch 3 episodes in a row on the treadmill, walking for roughly 2 ½ hours straight. I could barely walk to my car when I was done with the episodes, but they were awesome and the exercise was fantastic. I lost almost 20 pounds watching that show. You don't have to give up entertainment, you just have to modify how you experience your entertainment. I love having a series that I am into so that I will spend more time on the treadmill. When I lift weights, I hit the lifting as hard as I can for four songs. I don't rest in between sets, and I just keep moving from machine to machine while jamming to whatever group I chose for my four song workout. Once the four songs are done, my ability to lift stuff is usually pretty much done as well, and that is my signal to walk it off while watching a great show.

People spend several hours a night watching TV shows or Netflix or Hulu or Sling or whatever other entertainment app is out there when you are reading this. Shift your consumption of the entertainment to coincide with building a better fortress of a body to ward off the things that deplete you. When your body is in shape, your mind works more effectively. When your body is out of shape, it seems to make sense to lay around and be annoyed that your body didn't get in shape on its own. I am past my mid-forties as I am writing this, and I can tell you that it is easy to justify skipping the workout. I travel regularly. I have a family. I have a big yard to take care of. I have excuses that I can use. But they are just that… excuses. The reality is that we have to simply decide. Mel Robbins, in her book The Five Second Rule, says to simply count backward from 5 to 4 to 3 to 2 to 1 and then launch your ass into action and get some shit done (Robbins, 2017). Get your ass in gear and live a full life and a long life as well. I want to see you at 100!

The concept of launching yourself out of bed can be a difficult one when you find yourself sluggish or depressed. One thing you might consider is partnering up with someone who will be relentless if you skip out on working out with them. I have found that hiring a trainer is a great idea to get started and then finding a fit friend who loves to push you is the perfect way to continue. You can play basketball, volleyball, lift weights, swim, or do whatever is best for you and your body. Just… DO!

The simple truth is that your success is truly about you. It is about the beliefs you have, the thoughts you think, the actions you take, and the results you get. When you align your mind, body, and emotions, you take the kind of actions that get you the results you desire for yourself. A measure of where you are in your alignment can be heard in the words that you use when you talk to yourself. Pay close attention to whether or not you are building yourself up when you talk in your head, or even out loud, to yourself. If you continuously put yourself down, you are out of sync with truth. Practice saying great things to yourself and about yourself when you practice self-talk. Dr. Phil was very wrong! IT IS ABOUT YOU!!!

3 Welcome To Fight Club

From the speech "Citizenship in a Republic" delivered at the Sorbonne, in Paris, France on April 23, 1910 by Theodore Roosevelt.

"It is not the critic who counts; not the man who points out how the strong man stumbles, or where the doer of deeds could have done them better. The credit belongs to the man who is actually in the arena, whose face is marred by dust and sweat and blood; who strives valiantly; who errs, who comes short again and again, because there is no effort without error and shortcoming; but who does actually strive to do the deeds; who knows great enthusiasms, the great devotions; who spends himself in a worthy cause; who at the best knows in the end the triumph of high achievement, and who at the worst, if he fails, at least fails while daring greatly, so that his place shall never be with those cold and timid souls who neither know victory nor defeat."

--Theodore Roosevelt

戦争 This is the Japanese symbol for "war." When I first started training in martial arts, I wanted to learn how to fight. I am fairly sure that most of the people who joined martial arts in my small town were doing so in order to prepare for the day they might have to fight. I was a fairly small guy… Okay a really small guy at 9 years old, and I already had bullies that I was dealing with. These guys had simply grown taller and gained more weight than me by that age. I was afraid of getting hurt by others, afraid of dogs, afraid of pain. I joined martial arts in order to find my inner strength and to be ready to fight whenever necessary. I was not aware of where the battle existed, though. I assumed the battle would always be a physical struggle to overcome a bully. The reality was, the battle was mostly inside of me. It was a battle to be willing to face my fears, to step into the arena of life, to be willing to get hit and kicked in the pursuit of something great.

By the time I had been in martial arts for 6 months, I had gotten more comfortable with kicking other people. I was quick and was able to dodge most punches and kicks that other people threw and would then counter and get my points. I did well in tournaments, but I had not really gotten over my fear at that point. Fast forward a few years and my instructor picked up on the idea that I was unwilling to get hit. He tied my hands behind my back and had me spar someone that was using both their hands and feet in the match. This was incredibly good for me because it introduced me to the idea that I would have to take a few licks in order to advance. I eventually became comfortable sparring and taking a few licks. I continued in martial arts and changed styles early in high school. I had studied three styles, including Muay Thai for a short while (1 year). As I developed more skills in fighting and defending myself, I began to experiment with the "confidence" factor to see how others responded. I would hold my hands out and walk toward them as they attacked. I would deflect some of their hits and simply step into others. I learned that I could take a lot of punishment when I was moving forward and would generally overpower the other person even when I was smaller than them. This attack model put me fully into the fight and helped me learn to channel my energy to the right places for the attack. I practiced by getting hit in the mid-section, face, and even in the legs in order to desensitize the nerves and get used to the blows.

What I found was that most people were completely freaked out by a guy being willing to get hit and kicked. They wondered what in the hell was wrong with me and often backed up. Most people are scared of the competition. This truth has served me well in business as well as in life. When you are willing to take it on the chin, then you are actually in the fight. When you are running around the ring and trying to simply avoid the blows, you may be in the ring, but you are not in the fight. Life is about being in the fight. It is about being willing to be rejected, pushed away, and competed with. Life is about stepping fully into the arena of life and moving forward no matter what is coming at you. You have to do some things that are scary until you have conditioned yourself to step into the fear instead of shrinking from it. The last thing we need in this world is one more person unwilling to fight for something great. We need fighters. We need people who find freedom in the glory of the challenge and who are willing to get their asses kicked from time to time in order to experience the thrill of battle. There is honor in the struggle. There is honor in the victory. There is honor and purity in the battle itself. There is even honor in the loss. Are you ready to do battle?

I am not picking a fight with you when I ask that question. I AM daring you to pick a fight with yourself, however. I am daring you to look directly into your soul and be willing to kick and punch and scream and get real with what is holding you back. If you are not who you wish to be and where you wish to be at this exact moment in life, then it is time to get out of the stands and into the arena. You have some battles that you must fight in order to become the fullest and most badass version of yourself possible. My question in the last paragraph was about whether or not you are ready. The real question is, ARE YOU WILLING TO LOSE IN ORDER TO BE IN THE BATTLE?

Your willingness to step into the fight and risk the death of the old version of self matters the most. You have a story about you that wraps up who you are and where you are right now. This story is the one that has kept you in the specific comfort zone you are currently in at this moment. Is that the zone that represents the highest version of self? No? I didn't think so. You have a next level and a next. When you battle with the old version of yourself, you are unraveling the story that has defined you up to this point and writing a new story. The new story at the next level up will give you greater success, greater joy, greater freedom, and greater financial resource. Let's begin kicking the old story's ass and constructing a new and better story for your life!

Cliffhangers
The Zone, The Cliff, and the Climb

The 1st Rule of Fight Club

The 1st rule of fight club is that we do not talk about fight club. The second rule of fight club is WE DO NOT TALK ABOUT FIGHT CLUB! I love the first two rules of fight club because they just beg you to break the rules. When I think about the movie Fight Club, I think about a bunch of guys who were disillusioned with where their lives had ended up. At one point, Tyler Durden even refers to the group as "slaves in white collars." People who have simply had enough of where they are will go out of their way to change, but only if the pain of the present is greater than the anticipated pain of the journey. You need to build up your pain to the point that you are no longer willing to accept where you have been because you know where you should be. As you enter this stage of change, talk to yourself regularly. You don't really need to talk to other people about it because it is very tempting to talk of the victimhood that exists in your version of reality as you are coming out of the muck. Give up the whiner version of yourself. When you are in the middle of kicking your own ass into shape, it is critical that you don't go around whining about what is wrong or how the world is out to get you, or how others might not like you. You are in charge of this fight. When Edward Norton, as the narrator, reflects on how the final fight scene reminded him of his first fight, he was reflecting on the first time he beat himself up in order to find the other version of himself that existed. This is definitely not an encouragement to seek out a split personality disorder. It is, however, a plea for you to reach deep inside of you and find the power that is you. By the end of the movie, Norton gets rid of Tyler Durden, his other personality, in order to live fully in the power that was him. Not everybody can do this on their own. Most people need another person to push them and encourage them and drive them toward the prize. This is what Brad Pitt did for Edward Norton in the movie. He was his relentless coach and sage who would not quit until Norton became the full version of himself. It is often a great idea to have a coach who will keep you from being a victim and keep you from whining. Each of us must deal with our shit.

For Your Reference…From Wikipedia… This is Tyler Durden explaining the eight rules of fight club to a group of men:

> *Gentlemen, welcome to Fight Club.* ***The first rule of Fight Club is: You do not talk about Fight Club. The second rule of Fight Club is: You do not talk about Fight Club.*** *Third rule of Fight Club: Someone yells "Stop!", goes limp, taps out, the fight is over. Fourth rule: Only two guys to a fight. Fifth rule:*

> *One fight at a time, fellas. Sixth rule: No shirts, no shoes. Seventh rule: Fights will go on as long as they have to. And the eighth and final rule: If this is your first night at Fight Club, you* ***have*** *to fight* (Wikipedia, n.d.).

My B.s. is killing my b.S. and that is total B.S.!

My (B.s.) belief system is often the very thing that kills my (b.S.) business strategy and that is total (B.S.) bullshit. Why don't you make the calls necessary to build your business? Why do you hide behind a bottle or a coffee cup or a façade when you should be demonstrating your greatness to the world? It is because at an emotional level, at the level of your beliefs in your subconscious mind, you don't believe that you deserve greatness. You believe that you deserve to lose the fight. Take a moment and write a letter on the next page to money and success. These two characters are cousins and they go together. Express how you feel about them and what they mean to you. Be honest and direct!

____

____

____

____

____

____

____

____

____

____

____

____

____

____

____

____

Our beliefs about money and success are the very things that are either attracting success or repelling it. Like you read about earlier with magnetic fields, your beliefs are the things that generate these fields. Dealing with what our actual beliefs and thoughts are about money and success will help to free us to become the people we wish to be in life. The following are a few of the thoughts that I had in my original letter to success and money.

> *Hey success. Hey money. I really like you guys but you sometimes scare the shit out of me. I wonder if you like me back because I chase you so often and you keep running away. It seems like every time you tell me that we*

are going to hang out, you snub your nose at me and even flip me off at times. You have potential customers get excited when we meet, and I envision our life together and then you take the potential customer away for no reason. They hang out with you, and I get left out on my own. I know we could be happy together, and I really think that life would be better if we were together, but I worry about being greedy like some of the people that are in a relationship with you. They are sometimes mean and arrogant while they are with you. I worry that I will go to hell if I have you because I was taught that you are the reason that people become evil, and yet those same people want more of you and want me to share you with them. Why is it you are so fun to have and seem to make life amazing when you are around and why is it you keep running away? I think we could be awesome together if we just work our problems out. Please stay with me for the rest of my life. Please!

You have to get real with what you believe about yourself, success, money, failure, and others. As you can see from the note I wrote to success and money, I had a weird and sort of jacked up relationship. We definitely had our issues. In many ways, I felt like success was a bully and a tease. I am not a fan of either bullies or teases. I had to face some of the bad programming I had been given as a kid. I doubt my parents meant to teach me that having money made you evil, but the message I got from those lessons in church was just that. I learned that rich people go to hell and money just created problems. I had to finally break down and learn that it isn't money that sends you to hell. In fact, many of the most godly men in the bible had a great deal of money. For me to deal with some of the baggage I was carrying around, I connected with successful people, researched the origin of the those bible verses, and really sat with the feelings of inadequacy that were haunting me. A few verses that I want to clear up for you if you have that same church background are…

NIV Version of Matthew 19:24 – Again I tell you, it is easier for a camel to pass through the eye of a needle than a rich man to enter the kingdom of heaven. The Aramaic language, the original language for the Christian religious text used strong emphasis in order to drive a point home. There are also a few things that are lost in translation. The "eye of a needle" sounds so freaking impossible to me. How the hell do you get a camel through the eye of a needle? I struggle to get a string through there! Right? Well, the eye of the needle was the gate to the city. There were fewer words to explain things at the time, so one set of wording might mean several things. In order for a camel to pass through the eye of the needle, it could not have its stuff strapped to its back and it had to lower itself to pass through. It was always easier for a camel to get into the city because someone would take the stuff off the camel. A person simply cannot define themselves by their stuff. If you are so attached to your image, your possessions, your stuff, that you can't let go, then you are stuck. The true definition of you is based on who you are from the inside out, not the outside in.

NIV Version of 1 Timothy 6:10 – For the love of money is the root of all kinds of evil. Some people, eager for money, have wandered from the faith and pierced themselves with many sorrows. We forget the "some" part of this verse. That is the first mistake made. Some people… It doesn't say all people! It only says some people have wandered from the faith. The second struggle we have is that money used to be other stuff. The original text called it mammon. Mammon is stuff. Again, a person cannot define themselves by their stuff and still find success. When the definition of self is based on the stuff you own, then you will have a tendency to make decisions that are out of harmony with your true identity. You are. You are you, and you are not defined by things. There is nothing wrong with having things as long as you know that your worth doesn't come from the stuff. Your value comes from within. When you embrace this truth, you vibrate at a different level. You vibrate in a way that stuff, success, money, all of this begins to chase you instead of you chasing it.

Acts 20:35 - … "it is more blessed to give than to receive." Paul stated that his brethren were to remember the words of Jesus, yet Jesus was never quoted as saying this in any of the other gospels. This verse had me believing that it was wrong to receive. This jacked up misinterpretation was the perfect way to get people who have stuff to give it to the church so they had more stuff and could build bigger buildings as well as give more stuff to people who don't have stuff. The problem is that this vantage point keeps victims as victims and creates a hero out of the church. Heroes have to have victims! What if something was lost in translation? The original version of this was more accurately translated as "it is more blessed to be able to give than to need to receive." When you change only a few words in this verse, it changes the meaning completely. If it is more blessed to be able to give, than it is to be in a position of need, then perhaps the lesson was that we needed to pursue success because that position of success is what we were designed for. We were designed for greatness, not for lack! After all, you cannot give what you do not already possess.

What if your story has been wrong about money? What if you were always supposed to be successful instead of being in lack? What if you were going against what Source, God, Universal Intelligence, or the Universe or whatever you wish to refer to Omnipotence as, when you did not find your path to success? What if your story has been wrong in the past? If you want to believe something great about money and success, can you? You get to choose what you believe. James Allen once said, "To think what one wishes to think is to think the truth." You were never called to shrink into darkness. The world is served by you shining your light, by living into your success and your greatness. The world is changed by those who are bold enough to let go of the wrong stories and write better ones. Money is a vehicle, but you are still the driver. Never forget that you are in control of what you do with money. If you are generous before having money, you will likely be very generous when you have lots of money. Money amplifies who a person is, just like the other stuff around the person. Be an amplified version of your awesome self!

I Don't Give a Shit What You Think

We are taught from a very early age that it is rude to not care what other people think about us. We are supposed to care if the other kids in our class like us. We are supposed to care if people look at us funny. We are supposed to care what is going on in the minds of the people around us because... we are taught that their opinion is what is real. This is one of the most crippling thoughts we have in life. We are inadequate in the eyes of others. If you are like me, you have met at least a few people in this world where you wondered what was wrong with them. Okay, I admit it, there have likely been thousands of those people in my life. I wondered what was wrong with the kid in elementary school who ate glue. I wondered what was wrong with the girl who sat in the corner a lot and seemed to be very happy doing so. I wondered what was wrong with the guy walking down the street talking to himself the other day. There is a very good chance you have wondered, or judged, or evaluated, or rolled your eyes at a few people as well. Regardless of my thoughts about those people, they were still there, doing their thing. My opinion seemed to not really matter at all to them. Then there are the people who dress crazy, perform antics to make others laugh, and generally go out of their way to be goofy enough to allow the others to be themselves without fear. Those are the people I truly admire and strive to be like. I want to be the kind of guy who is so confident that I get to be myself even when the "haters gonna hate." Don't you?

As I began writing this book with its crass title, I wondered what some of the people in my life would say about me. I thought about some of the folks I know who do NOT behave with complete reverence for all that is holy… unless other people are watching. I thought about the people who like to bash others for doing things out of the ordinary. I thought about the people who don't like cursing because, well, for whatever reason they don't like it. I had to face myself in the mirror and ask whether or not this was a book that needed to be written. The answer was a clear "Hell Yes!"

Until you get past worrying what others think of you, you will never be able to fully pursue the life you desire. When I first began writing, I threw away the introduction to book 1 over 50 times in a 9 year window. I would write it and then worry about how it would be evaluated and throw it away. I would write it again and throw it away again. I finally had a friend, Elaine, who confronted me on my B.s. about whether or not I was a writer. It was her push to simply write because I was a writer, not because others might read my books, that made the biggest difference. That was huge for me. I learned to let go of what people might think and focus more on who I was and how to fully express myself to others. This is not the absence of fear, though.

Fear is ever present, staring us in the eyes and asking us who the hell we really are. George Orwell once said…

> "Writing a book is a horrible, exhausting struggle, like a long bout with some painful illness. One would never undertake such a thing if one were not driven on by some demon whom one can neither resist nor understand."

This is the struggle of virtually every creative type out there. They bobble between the fear of rejection from others and the fear of torment from something inside of them. When they finally stand up to both sides of reality and lay claim to the muse taunting them with a dialogue that must be transmuted into writing, or art, or some form of expression, they finally care about the right things. They must learn to not give a shit about the voices of others who say they are not enough or lack the education or talent. It is the voice inside of them, pushing them relentlessly toward expression, in the end, that matters the most.

Stop running your life based on whether or not people will like you. You have not made your cold-calls because people whom you have never met might not like you or might reject you. You have not asked that woman/girl/man/boy out who is charming and funny and makes you feel fantastic when you are in their presence because she/he might reject you. You have not started that business because you might fail at it. Your great epiphany needs to be… by not taking a chance, you are choosing guaranteed failure. Yes, you might fail if you try. Yes, others might not like you the way you want to be liked. Who gives a shit? Really! At the end of your life, if the popular kid in school who will likely have the best years of his/her life before the age of 19 didn't like you, are you really missing out on anything? NO!!! You miss out on greatness when you choose to shrink from your glory.

The world does not need another coward, one who sheds the skin of opportunity in pursuit of the comfort of a slow and pointless death with judgment. The world needs greatness. The world needs you to not give a shit what the world thinks of you. For then, the world will pursue you. Success will seek you out. Money will flow abundantly to you. This is how magnetism works. You are either the piece of metal being pulled one way or another, or you are the magnet. Magnets don't chase down pieces of metal to attract. They simply pulse their greatness out and the pieces of metal respond to them. Shine as the person you are. Don't Give A Shit What Anyone Else Thinks Of Your Glory! Then, they will follow you anywhere you wish to lead.

Until you get punched in the face...

"Everybody's got a plan until they get punched in the face." Mike Tyson - One of the greatest face punchers in history.

When I was a teenager, Mike Tyson was better than Rocky Balboa (fictional character created by Sylvester Stallone). Tyson was an incredible fighter and was managed by Don King (fictional character created by Don King). If you got up to grab some popcorn in the first 20 seconds of a fight, it is likely that you would have missed the entire fight. He knocked guys out so fast they didn't know what hit them. They had a plan on how to beat Tyson. I am quite sure they trained and believed they could beat Tyson. A couple of people did, but most just hit the mat with the kind of thud that says, "That was a bad idea." We used to talk about how much money it would take for us to fight Tyson. I never thought I could beat Tyson, but I did say I was willing to get in the ring with him. Sadly, King never called my manager (fictional character created just now) to arrange the fight. My martial arts tournament wins apparently did not qualify me for a multi-million dollar ass-whooping. The point was not whether I could beat Tyson or whether my friends could beat him. The point was what it would take for us to get in the ring and go toe to toe with one of the greatest boxers ever.

When I was training on a regular basis, and fighting 5 to 6 days per week for over an hour a day, it did something for my confidence. I learned that I could get punched in the face by life and still have the ability to get back up again. It wasn't about winning every time I stepped onto the mat. It was about being willing to step on the mat and get my ass handed to me or do the same to the other guy. One of the challenges that Tyler Durden handed out in Fight Club was to pick a fight with another person and then lose. The guys who were a part of Fight Club would go to the mall or walk down the street or simply harass others at work and then lose the fight. As Durden points out in the movie, normal people avoid getting into fights. We are taught from an early age not to fight. I am not advocating picking fights. I am simply illustrating a point that you cannot ever win a fight that you are afraid to enter. Whether you are afraid of what others will think or afraid of failing or afraid of the fight, you are giving a shit about the wrong things. My hope for you is the same as my plan for me. I will continue to live into who I am. I will write. I will speak. I will train. I will coach. Those are the things that are inside of me and chase me down relentlessly unless I listen to them and heed their call. I am not afraid of them. They are a part of me. I care about living fully as myself. I do not, however, give a shit about what others think.

Practical Application… Look yourself in the mirror and tell yourself… "I don't give a shit what you think of me." Then, imagine each of the people in your life holding you back because you care too deeply about their opinion. Visualize them right in front of you and tell them, "I don't give a shit what you think of me." I am not advocating that you practice being mean to others. When you are mean, you are attempting to get others to care what you think of them. Why should they give a shit if you don't? This exercise is for you. Make your decisions less on what others might think and more on what you know to be your truth. Your truth shall set you free!

4 F.U. Fundamental Understanding

"Life changes when a person accepts radical responsibility for all of who they are… their thoughts, emotions, actions, words, and ultimately their place in the world."
--Jody Holland, Self-quoter and fully accepting of that

Diaper Change

To transform anything, you have to be aware of the shit that is hidden and know when it is time to change. I am the proud father of two young ladies. When they were infants, I participated in the diaper change process and remember several occasions when I wondered if anything so vile could really have come out of something so adorable. Based on my stinging eyes and gag reflex from the smell, I went with yes. Transformation requires the acknowledgement of pain that exists in the moment and the desire to move past the pain. People will often wallow in the pain and suffering in order to demonstrate to the world that they are a victim of… whatever they can claim at the moment. We must choose one of two pathways for any decision. Do we stay where we are or move to a new place?

There is often pain in any choice that we make. There is pain in taking a new path, and there is pain in staying on the same path we are currently on. As we attempt to make our decision about which way to choose, we weigh the intensity of the pain with either choice. The problem that most people have in weighing out their pain is in looking at the short-term pain versus the long-term gain. For example, when you were in 8th grade and had to do a book report, it was easy to justify playing outside or playing a video game instead of doing the book work. It was easy until the night before the report was due. Then, many 8th graders would stay up late skimming the book or googling key points to the book instead of putting in the work to do it right the first time.

We do the same thing with work, working out, starting a business, getting six-pack abs, or any creative endeavor. Steven Pressfield, in The War of Art, talks about the dragons that one must slay in order to move forward on these endeavors (Pressfield, 2012). I would refer to them as demons we must kill. One friend calls them the black dogs from procrastination hell. Whatever name you give to the reasons you would rather mow the yard or mend the fence than write a book or paint a painting, the reality remains the same. Procrastination is simply the allocation of psychological pain management techniques. Creating a new model for overcoming this shit is really important in order to avoid the diaper rash of staying stuck where you are.

Step 1: Take the damn diaper off! You have a protective system you have created that allows you to use excuses instead of moving forward. I only know this because I have had multiple systems throughout my life and every person I have coached has their own system. These diapers of disappointment are full of the shitty excuses and people who protect you from having to take a risk. They make it okay for you to do something other than your great endeavor. They make it okay that you have not owned yourself and your choices. They make it okay that you are stuck where you are. It isn't their fault, though. You have asked them to be your protection. You strapped the diaper on and asked them to help fasten it. Only you can rip the Velcro closure off and get ready to clean yourself up. Stop accepting ANY excuses from yourself or others for why you have not taken the right action yet. Stop being a victim. You have to get rid of that protection that makes the excuses okay and you are the one who put them in place.

Step 2: You have to clean yourself up. You, like virtually everyone else I have met (me included), have some things to deal with. You have made choices that have made your credit bad, put you in a place where you can't afford your rent, borrowed money and purchased things you should not have, and/or not done the work that was required to be successful. There aren't any excuses that make this okay. I recently listened to a speech by Arnold Schwarzenegger where he described the work it took for him to come to the United States and escape the economic depression of Austria post World War II. He worked out 5 hours per day, went to school 4 hours per day, and worked at his job as a brick layer and foreman for 8+ hours per day. He did this 6 days a week! This made me realize the one thing that often keeps people from finding success. One of his steps in his success formula was to work your ass off! Most people are simply not willing to put in the work. They want to work up to 8 hours a day and then want to sit around and watch TV or do something mindless that requires no effort on their part. At the end of their lives, they look back and say they simply didn't have time. They will blame the economy or their parents or their spouse or the lack of enough time in the day. What?! Don't they have the same amount of time as everyone else? Yes they do! If another person can figure it out, you can figure it out. Get rid of any excuse you would use to put things off. Any time you find yourself wanting to make up some lame-ass excuse for not doing what is required of you, say the following proverb out loud…

THERE ARE NO EXCUSES!

Step 3: Put on a new protective layer that keeps out the excuses and keeps your momentum safe. Start each day with gratitude for the things you have in your life. Then, map out at least three things you intend to accomplish that day. Next, ensure your calendar is mapped out to keep out the bad stuff and keep you on track. At the end of the day, review what you have accomplished and ensure that you kept yourself on track. Set up your day to support your progress. As an entrepreneur, this is one of the most difficult things I must do. It is easy for the people around me to think that I can do anything I want. Often, people will assume you are already rich if you own a business. Typically, these people are in non-profits or have never ventured into the entrepreneurial ocean. Create rules that keep you safe. One example of a rule I have is that I can only be on 2 non-profit boards at a time. When a third non-profit executive asks me to be on their board, I simply quote the rule to them and apologize that I will not be able to help them. They accept it and I get back to work! Rules are very seldom questioned even if you are the one that made up the rules. Take a minute and write out a few rules to protect you in your pursuit of success.

____

____

____

____

The Spiral and The Climb

As we grow and develop, we pass through the same challenges over and over again. It is likely that you notice the same freak out sessions in your life, related to going broke or not knowing what the hell you are supposed to do next. Yours may be different than mine, but of the 100 or so entrepreneurs and business leaders I have interviewed have reported, they each have something that gets them rattled.

Success

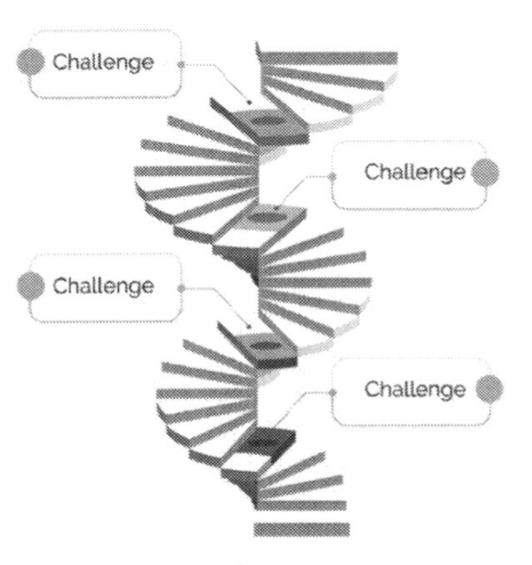

Start of Your Journey

One of the struggles that many people face as they move up in life is the "imposter syndrome." This is the feeling that you don't deserve to be where you are and that you are going to be found out soon. It is being afraid that others will figure out that you are winging it, guessing, and generally trying to find your way to the top of the spiral without falling back to the beginning. One of my personal favorite freak out sessions tends to be related to thinking the sky is going to fall and everything I have worked so hard to build is going to come crashing down around me. For years, I have produced multiple six figures in training, speaking, and coaching. Yet, despite the history of demonstrating I am not an imposter, I still wonder why people want to listen to me. I know I am not alone on this. CEOs, HR directors, entrepreneurs, and even mid-level managers have told me how they think that they have been promoted beyond their skills. Laurence J. Peters even had a principle on the subject. Peters stated that people are systematically promoted beyond their level of competence. We get promoted to the next level and then we learn how to handle that level. That is the essence of the spiral and the climb.

As we spiral up toward the top, if we have not learned to face the challenge, we tend to crumble and have to restart the climb over and over again. It is in facing the challenge, the demon, the black dog, or the devil that we learn to master the next level of the game. Life and success can be seen as a game we must master. The challenge is… every new level attained creates a new level to attain. In the journey, we find our joy. In the struggle, we find our strength. If you were to go through life and nothing challenged you, what would be your reason for growth? You wouldn't have one. I am not suggesting that life needs to be impossibly hard. I am suggesting that we should face the challenges and growth opportunities with an attitude of confidence and gratefulness. These are the things that mold and shape us into the greatness intended for our lives. Without the problems, there would be no growth. Without the growth, there would be no next level of the climb toward success. Without the next level, we would not live into our potential. Be thankful for the challenge. Embrace the struggle toward success. Face it with the attitude of a warrior who is getting better at his/her craft every single day. Screw thinking about the imposter. The imposter is the version of you who is too scared to try. The warrior never backs down from the fight.

I think about the movie with the Spartans, where a few hundred men were willing to face off with thousands of men as their enemies. At least one of them had to be thinking… "What the hell are we doing here?" But that is what made the story great. I know they were scared at least at a gut level. Yet, they chose to step into the climb toward greatness. They chose to not back down from the crazy looking dude who called himself a god-king. They chose to fight their way to the top no matter what. It is that kind of reckless abandon, that kind of commitment, that kind of zeal that changes the world. Are you committed to the climb? Are you committed to fighting your way through the struggles that attack your mind? Are you ready to face the challenges that can make you great once you have overcome them? If you are committed, you can begin to build that greatness in yourself. You can begin to climb with confidence and build skill upon skill to perfect who you were meant to be.

Scaffolding

We build scaffolding to move ourselves up in life. Just like the learning theory that says we build upon previous lessons and previous wins, we do the same thing in life. As we seek out the lessons to build on, we are mastering a new self. Each new level of scaffolding we put in place raises our ability to succeed. Each new problem overcome represents a new level of capability in our lives. You will not be the same person in six months if you are building off the lessons learned in life. You cannot be the same person next year if you are truly facing and overcoming challenges. I am not saying you will alter your personality necessarily. I am, however, saying you will alter your beliefs about self, the world, and success. You must operate with a mindset that says you can learn new skills because you have demonstrated learning in the past. You cannot believe in the idea of stagnation. Your characteristics are not fixed. They are malleable, pliable, and workable. You can reshape yourself into anything you wish.

When I was 15 years old, my family moved from the small town I had grown up in to a small city. That was a move from 3,000 people to over 100,000 people. I decided to recreate myself into the guy I wanted to be instead of the set of labels I had accepted from others in the small town. I changed the way I talked, dressed, carried myself, and interacted with the world around me. That was my first real experience with how easy it was to be anyone I wanted to be. I was accepted by the groups that I thought were the right ones for social standing because I presented myself as one of them. It still fascinates me how easily a person can be who they wish to be if they simply get rid of the old version of self. I studied what the group was like and visualized myself in the group before I even moved to the new city. This gave me perspective that would last for the rest of my life. I could do anything I wanted and have anything I wanted if I was first willing to be, or exist as the version of a person that did and had those things.

We have to be willing to start at the bottom and work our way to the top, following the steps of change that make change stick. Each day, you see yourself as the person who already does and has the things you desire. If you desire riches, then embrace how awesome rich people are and embrace yourself as a rich person. You will never have that which you despise or hate. If you hate people who have money, you will never allow yourself to be a person with financial resources. You are your cause for lack when you have disdain for others. Love the fact that other people have already made their fortunes. Love the fact that success leaves clues, that you can study people who have come before you and understand the scaffolding of success they used. Love the fact that they have outlined the daily choices you must make in order to succeed at the same level as them. Be willing to make the climb, make the choices, make the sacrifices necessary to achieve success. If you are willing to start at the bottom and construct yourself into the man or woman necessary, you will find success. In The Science of Getting Rich Wallace

Wattles outlined that when one follows the formula of riches, one is sure to get rich (Wattles, 1910). If you are not willing to build the scaffolding that raises you up, to follow a formula for success, you are not going to find success. Make the choice to be the greatest version of self possible! Make the choice to let go of the past and embrace a formula for succeeding.

Voodoo and A Hex

I published a book called Faces of Reality that taught people how to look at a person's face and understand the psychology of who they are. On a number of occasions, I have been told not to try that "voodoo" stuff on the person I am with. Knowing how to see into the psyche of another person gives you a great advantage. The challenge is generally less about being able to see the other person and more about being able to truly see what we are doing to ourselves. The crazy things that we accept in our minds are what limit us from reaching our potential. One of the hexes I have found in my own life is that of thinking I get sick whenever I slow down. This goes back several generations in my family. My grandfather retired and had to have bypass surgery a few months later. My dad retired and got cancer. The message my mind constructed was that men in my family who stop working move quickly towards the grave. I have experienced getting sick on the first day of vacation more than a dozen times. I put myself in a position to shut my body down when I am not living into my work purpose. The truth and my truth are not the same thing. My truth was that I was doomed to get sick and die if I didn't work. The truth was that I pushed myself so hard that I needed to be forced to rest and recover.

It is easy to put a hex on yourself. You can put a good hex or a bad hex on you, but it is likely that you are hexing yourself in one way or another. When we say things like "something always crashes as soon as things start going my way," we are hexing ourselves and redirecting our Reticular Activating System to seek out a crash when we accept things as going our way. Athletes have lucky socks they might not ever wash and they wear every game. People have a lucky pen, lucky shoes, lucky underwear, or even a ritual they perform before a big event. I am not saying there is anything necessarily wrong with doing things that set you in a state of success. I am, however, saying that we often don't think about what we are doing or what it is doing to us. We simply act in a certain direction because we have formed the habit of doing so. Think about some of the things you have been telling yourself for years that have limited your success. "Nobody in my family wins at life," or "I never catch a break," or "life is unfair and never unfair in my favor," are all examples of hexes that we put on ourselves for no reason. These types of statements direct our minds to fulfill the hex.

The power of a hex, the power of voodoo, the power of anything is in the faith back of the belief. When we have faith that something is going to come true, we seek out ways to validate the belief. You can just as easily believe you are lucky as believing you are unlucky. According to Psychology Today, people's beliefs about luck fall into one of two categories. They either believe that luck is stable and predictable or fleeting and unpredictable. What is fascinating is that one's belief in good luck has a positive impact on their willingness to move themselves forward in life.

> "People who saw their luck as stable tended to have a significantly *higher* drive to succeed than those who viewed it as transitory." (Dowden PhD, 2014)

It fascinates me to think about the good or bad hexes we put on our own lives. Think about some of the things you could choose to believe about your own life that would support your success. How could you look at luck, good fortune, or a positive hex on your life as something that was stable and working continuously in your favor? What would you have to believe about luck to see it as always on your side?

In order to feel lucky, I would have to believe…

____

____

____

____

If I wanted to believe I was lucky on a consistent basis and I wanted to accept the belief about myself written above, could I?

☐ Yes ☐ No

Do I want to believe I am lucky?

☐ Yes ☐ No

The crazy part of all this is knowing that luck has more to do with the energy we put off than the energy being projected toward us. Every person I have worked with has had a belief about the way life has gone. Some believe in random chance. Some believe in stable good or bad luck. Some believe that life is a struggle and one must continuously fight against other people in order to succeed. Whatever their belief, it tended to play out in their life.

People make remarks like, "this place was built on an Indian burial ground, and that is why shit goes sideways." When we believe in superstition, it works. So, why not use this to our advantage. Why not create a rallying cry and move things forward? Why not get rid of the old voodoo and make some positive voodoo. This is done by becoming a master influencer and learning to plant ideas, cultivate possibilities, and direct the flow of energy. Much of this direction has to do with our own minds first! We must choose to believe in the good, and we must use our words wisely. Incantations, hexes, voodoo, healing, or any other form of directed belief starts with what we believe, then moves to what we think.

These two things determine what we do and ultimately what we achieve. Whether you realize it or not, you have been conditioning your success for most of your life. The things you tell yourself about your interaction with the world, the things you tell yourself about your place in the world, and the beliefs you adopt about luck and happenstance are all influencing the direction the world goes in relation to you.

In 1905, Walter Wintle published a poem titled "Thinking." In the poem, he explains that it is in one's thoughts that they find success or failure or struggle or triumph. Read the poem aloud a couple of times and consider your own thoughts in relationship to the world around you.

If you think you are beaten, you are;
If you think you dare not, you don't.
If you'd like to win, but you think you can't,
It is almost certain - you won't.

If you think you'll lose, you've lost;
For out in this world we find
Success begins with a fellow's will
It's all in the state of mind.

If you think you're outclassed, you are;
You've got to think high to rise.
You've got to be sure of yourself before
You can ever win the prize.

Life's battles don't always go
To the stronger or faster man;

But sooner or later the man who wins
Is the one who thinks he can!
(Wintle, 1905)

What is it you think about you? Become intentional about the manner in which you look at yourself. Choose to see the good in you before you see any negative. Choose to believe that luck is on your side. Choose to believe that the universe is an abundant place, full of joy and love and desire to bring good into your life. Choose to believe in yourself and the world will respond in your favor!

Twin Peaks

There will always be a valley between the peaks. You have to embrace the challenges in order to make yourself stronger. The valleys you face are not the world trying to destroy you. It is the universe reaching into your life and helping you exercise your will to win, to continue, to grow stronger. The valley is the struggle and challenge you need in order to develop your muscles of success. Don't be upset about struggles. Embrace them, for every person who achieved greatness became great in the valley and was seen on the peak. When life seems to be coming at you, choose your attitude wisely. I am a fairly athletic person. I like to lift weights. I have done martial arts for the vast majority of my life. I stretch on a regular basis and work to stay in good shape. All of this is work, though. You don't become a great martial artist by playing martial arts video games. You might understand some of the basic principles from the game, but getting into the ring and being willing to actually fight another person is much different than circle, circle, triangle, left paddle, forward, or whatever combination would be a great attack with the game controller.

We need struggle! We need the chance to grow ourselves into a stronger, more confident version of self than we were yesterday. When I began sparring (controlled fighting in martial arts), I lacked the confidence in my ability to defend myself in a real-life situation. The more I sparred, the more I believed I could take care of myself should anything happen. I was more confident in my fighting ability with each conquered struggle. For both my brown and black belt tests, I had to fight multiple attackers at the same time. These were people who had already achieved black-belt status. And… they were good! I did not win the fight. Winning wasn't the point. The point was to see if I would step into the fight and give it all I had. For my black-belt test, I progressed from 5 one-on-one fights up to a five-on-one. The last fight was for points and would continue until I scored two points. A point was scored by a well-executed body blow or shot to the head. If I had not fought thousands of times before the day of my test, I would have completely freaked out. I knew, however, that I could score a couple of points in a fight like this. I picked my target on the end of the line of 5, spun backwards toward them, faked a low kick and performed an upper cut to the chin making great contact. That was point 1. The second point was a spinning back side kick to the other side of the line toward a rather large individual (muscular) where I caught him mid-air in the ribs with my heal. Those were my two points and the fight was done.

I was thankful for all of the valleys, the fights, the struggles I had experienced up to that point. They prepared me for moving back up to the peak. Consider the problems you have faced in your life. Think about how they have prepared you to be better at life now. Think about the lessons you have learned as a result of the struggle. You are not beaten because you took a few hits. You are only beaten if you refuse to embrace the struggle as a lesson and a preparation for the next battle. What will you choose for your life? Will you choose to see the lesson, to believe in your own luck, to find a way to win? Or, will you choose to believe that you are beaten before the battle begins? The choice is yours! Every challenge is a chance to grow.

A Trance State

Mastering meditation puts you in a place where you can experience your other self and get in touch with both peace and power. You have to breathe to live so it makes sense to breathe correctly in order to live correctly. As we get older, more stressed out, more focused on what is happening in the world around us, we breathe less, are more shallow in our breaths, and less intentional about keeping our lungs moving in the right direction. Before any big event, it is ideal for you to take a minute or two and simply breathe. Breathe in through your nose and out through your mouth. Practice expanding and contracting the top of your lungs, the middle of your lungs, and the bottom of your lungs. How you hold your arms will determine which part of your lungs naturally expands and contracts. When you are seated and your arms are down, breathe in while expanding your belly. Then, raise your arms to shoulder height, with your palms facing down and your elbows bent in so that your hands are close to your armpits. Finally, place the palms of your hands on your upper back with your elbows up in the air and near your ears. This will expand lower, then middle, then upper lung as you breathe in and out.

Meditation begins with clearing your mind and shifting your focus to something specific. Being in the zone, or a trance state, is actually about narrowing your focus to be targeted to something very specific. Focusing on your breathing is a practice that allows you to get rid of many of the things floating around in your head. Before going into a big meeting, making an important presentation, or having an important client interaction, take a few minutes to clear your mind by focusing on breathing properly. Once you have cleared your mind, while still focusing on proper breathing, pull the idea of success in the interaction into the forefront of your mind. See only the event that is about to happen. See it in vivid detail and see it going perfect. When you keep the focus on the singular event and the perfect execution of the event, all of the valleys you have been through and the lessons you have learned will shape your approach. You see the lessons and know confidently that you will be able to handle anything that comes your way. See the event playing through and see the perfect outcome on the other side. Strip away the things that might be distractions and stay focused on seeing yourself succeed.

The zone, the trance state, or whatever you like to call it, is a way of narrowing your focus to allow in only that which serves you best. Stay in this focus as you get out of your car, or head out of your office toward the meeting. Most of the problems imagined in this world are just that. They are imagined. Most of the successes imagined in this world are just that as well. They are imagined. Nothing is achieved in this world without first being conceived in the mind. In addition to practicing this quick meditation practice before a big meeting, it is a great idea to hold the thought and feeling of your life going perfect as you drift off to sleep. In order for your subconscious mind to do what it needs to do to create success for you, you must let go of the stress and struggles from the day. When our thoughts and feelings are in alignment, our world falls into place. It cannot be just thoughts, though. Man is not capable of success without the addition of feeling mixed with thoughts and backed by faith in a vision of success. Your formula for success as you walk through this life is to have the belief/faith that the universe is abundant and seeks only good for you, to think thoughts of success for your life, and to feel success every chance you get. It is critically important that you intentionally feel success, think success, and believe in your success as you drift off to sleep. The reason for this is that the subconscious mind is most susceptible to suggestion in this drowsy state. You are naturally in a trance state, accepting of suggestion as you drift off to sleep. Make sure to program the right things in your mind and your life. After all, your success is predicated on your belief about your success mixed with your thoughts and feelings about you. All of this is simply a choice you make. Choose wisely!

5 Up Yours: Up Your Ownership Mentality and Create an Intrapreneurial Culture

"The biggest adventure you can take is to live the life of your dreams."
--Oprah Winfrey

Own It or Get Owned

Throughout our lives, we are either being pulled in one direction or another by the world around us, or we are doing the pulling. In life, we pass through phases of perception that relate to the manner in which we experience life. Each of the four phases represents a perception that we experience related to life itself. The great thing, as well as the horrible thing, about perception is that we experience perception as truth. William James, considered the father of American Psychology, said, "That which I perceive is my reality." Truth is simply perception accepted. It isn't absolute. As we journey through our lives, pursuing success, we often find the very thing that holds us back is the perception about how success is attained.

When we are born, we experience life as ourselves, without regard or reference to the outside world. We do not consider how our parents will feel when we scream in the middle of the night because we are hungry or have just soiled ourselves. We simply know that life is not going the way we want it to, so we pitch a fit. Some people stay in this completely self-absorbed state throughout their lives. They are unaware of how their actions and behaviors impact people around them. They pitch fits, cry, moan, whine, and generally act like babies until they get their way. I am thankful that I only dated one person in my life who behaved in that manner. That was a very short-lived relationship.

As we move along the perceptive continuum, we move from life happening as us to life happening to us. The majority of people, by the age of 7-ish, will begin to feel that life is happening to them. This would indicate that they want to have conscious processing but feel that it is not an option for them. They feel that circumstances in their lives are what dictate their life to them. Based on what has been reported by Napoleon Hill, Jonathan Heston, and a host of other authors on success, the vast majority of people believe they are a victim of their circumstances. They feel that they have little to no control over what goes on in their lives. Think about conversations you have listened to where people explain the things that are wrong in their lives. Do they explain how they made this bad choice or that bad choice and, as a result, their life is not going the right direction? Or, do they explain how this person or that person or the government did something to them that has prevented them from living the life that they desired? I have met very few people that simply own their own choices. I think some people would freak out if they had to wake up every day and own every single choice they made. Our society has conditioned us that things are not our fault. If you had a bad childhood, that is your parents' fault. If you are broke, it is the economy. If you are unhappy, it is society or your significant other, or something along those lines. Really? That is the philosophy of the person who doesn't own their choices or their thoughts. Life moves so much smoother when we move ourselves out of this phase and into owning our choices!

The third phase of perception is to believe that life happens by me. You can no longer accept that your circumstances or anyone around you is in charge of your success or failure. This is the point when life begins to actually go in the right direction. I have found that owning my thoughts, my attitudes, my emotions, my day, and my choices in every given moment lead me to success on a consistent basis. It doesn't mean that I will never have struggle in my life. It means that anytime struggle shows up, I look at the choices I have made up to that point and make a new choice to get out of the trouble. I don't blame the economy, my parents, my spouse, or anything / anyone else for the place I am in life. I choose. I choose everything about my day. I own my day! The question that I ask myself is…

In this situation, with the resources that I have, what can I do to make things better?

That question doesn't allow me to look to someone else. It requires me to look within. It requires me to own me. It is about not asking why or when will questions anymore. Why and when will questions would be…

- Why is this happening to me?
- Why didn't my parents better prepare me?
- Why is the economy bad?
- When will marketing get their act together so I can make sales easier?
- When will administration start appreciating me?
- When will those other people do that thing that I have convinced myself is making it impossible to succeed?

Asking questions that support owning my next choice and moving myself forward position me for success. It is in the final phase where we flow back and forth from life happening by me to life happening through me that we experience the greatest ownership of self and the greatest success. It is a continuous remembrance to stay focused on being willing to receive greatness from the universe. It is in this decision that we enter into the final phase of life happening through us.

As we accept that life happens through us, this is the portion of life where we give up the illusion of struggle and embrace the truth that God, Source, the Field of Potentiality, or whatever you want to refer to as the great deity, has our back. When life is happening through us, we experience the joy and ease of success that we have hoped for. The reason we experience success is that we are already a success in our beliefs, thoughts, and actions. Success is the natural state of someone who clearly defines themselves as a success.

James Allen, in As A Man Thinketh, taught that man never becomes that which he wishes to be. He becomes that which he is already aware of being. When life is flowing through us, it is the awareness of self as its best version that matters. When you think of you at your best, are you able to accept that as your truth? When you see that vision, does it bring you peace or does it bring you anxiety? We must visualize ourselves at our best, accepting this as our truth, feeling as if it has already happened, and then the universe delivers that truth to us. Remember from the magnetic fields section, we attract that which we are, not that which we wish for.

From Shit to Shinola

Your world is one decision away from better and one decision away from worse, and now is decision time. I heard a speaker in Galveston, Texas say that he has always had the capacity to take a bad situation and make it infinitely worse. He said that in reference to some choices he made as a very young man after his parents both passed in a short amount of time. He is a humorist as well as a motivator, but he made a great point. So often, when things seem to be headed to the toilet, people make choices that amplify the problem instead of eliminating the problem. This is often because we are making decisions from a fear-based stance instead of from a confidence-based stance. It is also related to the challenge of making decisions with our emotions versus our cognitive processes (intellect).

I have been coaching business owners and top executives for almost 2 decades now and have heard a consistent comment when it comes to the problems that exist for them. "If we could just get rid of emotions, this business would be great." If we could just get rid of emotions.... That is an interesting thought, but I don't think getting rid of emotions would be a good idea at all. What those executives actually mean is that they would like to get rid of the negative emotions. The positive emotions pull people toward higher levels of performance and enhance the experience of the venture. The positive emotions are what make things worthwhile. The key to success has nothing to do with getting rid of emotions. The key is knowing which emotions to flush and which emotions to keep.

By dealing with the mental sewage holding you back, you are positioning yourself for success. You can cling to the things that make life enjoyable. You cannot, however, hold on to the crap in your mind and expect to have the clarity required to win at this game called business. I was on a call with several other entrepreneurs recently, and one of the folks was talking about "the thing" that is holding them back.

It was a story that she had repeated to herself most of her life and that she was trying to let go of. I shared with her a story I had heard related to the easy way to capture a monkey.

As I was told, to capture a monkey in the jungle, you simply cut a hole in a wooden box large enough for the monkey to put its hand through and have something that is either shiny or enticing inside of the box. The monkey will come up to the box, see the desirable object inside of the box, reach in his/her hand in order to retrieve it, and then get its hand stuck because it is now closed around an object large enough to make its hand too big for the hole. The monkey will struggle to get its hand out of the box but will not let go of the object. The "monkey hunter" can simply walk up to the monkey and bop it on the head or put it in a net, and voila, you have captured a monkey. All the monkey really had to do was let go of the object and run away to be free. It would have been so simple, but it apparently was not easy.

I think we do the same thing with our lives. We are stuck in the idea of holding on to our stories, our past, our excuses, or whatever shiny object allows us to not succeed and still blame something outside of us, instead of simply letting go and moving on. When you are holding on to the excuses you have about your lack of success, that is the mental sewage killing your success. Let go of any excuse. Let go of your ego. Let go of your need to be right or your need for others to see you in a certain light. To live the life of your dreams, you embrace the truth that you need nothing, and you have nothing to prove to anyone, anywhere, at any time. You are enough!

One of my hippie friends was telling me that the best mushrooms are grown inside piles of shit. They create the best psychotropic effect and experience. I would never have thought of digging through piles of shit to find my escape, but the idea that people are willing to dive into shit in order to find their way out of their shit is kind of fascinating. We spread manure on our gardens to grow healthy vegetables. We mix manure with other things to create amazing fertilizer which helps to feed the masses. What if we looked at the shit in our own lives and started sifting through the experiences to find the glory?

Your problems are not the end of you. They are the things that make you stronger, more prepared, and better equipped for greatness. Your problems help to refine you, but not to define you. To move from shit to shinola, you simply have to embrace the idea that problems are gold nuggets of opportunity. They are the chance you have been given to hone your skills, enhance your status in life, and find a new pathway to success. The only problem with problems is to think that having problems is a problem. The manner in which we process having a problem determines whether it is shit or fertilizer. Fertilizer grows us into higher potential, but it is based on aligning our thoughts about the problem (I know that I will find a way) and our feelings about the problem (I am really good at solving problems and feel accomplished when I do). What are the thoughts that you could choose to have about problems if you wanted to see problems as opportunities and as a positive?

____

____

____

____

Going Mental

What does it mean to be an entrepreneur? What does it mean to think like a successful entrepreneur? These questions haunted me as I began my journey to success. In my mind, I originally thought that the simple act of going into business would land me lots of clients, success, money, fame and glory. The thoughts of an entrepreneur, or anyone for that matter, are everything. You are not guaranteed or owed anything. I think one of the great frustrations of our society is in their thinking about what is owed to them. When you walk into any situation and expect nothing from others, you simply take action. Giving up the need for someone else to do something before you act frees you to simply move forward. If you think you are fully responsible for yourself, your actions, your results, then you accept your ultimate responsibility in life. Examine your thoughts about the world around you. Look deep into your mind in order to understand who you see yourself as in this world.

As a human, your thoughts are more of a crystal ball than a mirror. When you look deep into the thoughts you have about life, money, love, success, etc., you see what your future will be. Your thoughts are the substance that create reality. Mind is the connection to Source that creates. But what is mind? Mind is you! You are not simply 6 trillion cells feverishly attempting to regenerate and survive. You are the vibrational energy of your thoughts holding together 6 trillion cells in the form that appears to be you. Out of your thoughts, you determine the reality of your existence. You create either good or you create bad. The circumstance is secondary to the thought and never the cause of the thought.

One of my entrepreneurial friends explained it this way. An entrepreneur is the person who can be told that there is a 1 in a million chance of achieving greatness and then immediately takes their family out to celebrate their odds. Entrepreneurs hone in on the 1, not the 999,999. They focus like a laser on the things they can control and the singular destination they have chosen. Their mind is vibrating at the "get back up and try again no matter what" level. They don't know how to back down. Even if they learned how to back down, they would forget that one thing as fast as possible. Your attitude is your choice. Your thoughts are your choice. Take them seriously!

You can't think your way out of the matrix. But you can think your way into success within the Matrix. In the movie, *The Matrix*, Neo is the main character and he is waiting to see the oracle. The room he is in is full of bright and talented people who hope to have something to offer the world. In a conversation with a young boy who is bending spoons, he is told…

"Do not bend the spoon with your mind. That is impossible. Instead, realize that there is no spoon and bend your mind."

Think about that. What if you embraced yourself in this space and simply owned your next move, every single time you have the chance to make a next move. If you are fully present and fully responsible for your thoughts in any given situation, you stop blaming others for the things that have not worked. There are way too many people who are trying to bend spoons with their mind. They are trying to get out of the Matrix, or this reality, and get someone else to be responsible for them. Lean into reality. Lean into your thoughts. Lean into the idea that you are radically responsible for yourself. There isn't any situation where someone else can do your thinking for you and you end up better off. You be responsible for you!

Feel Me Up

The feelings that we feel are real to us. In fact, they create a different version of reality for us, in us, and through us. Feelings are the secret ingredient to this soup of a life we live in. When we feel as if the world is out to get us, we search for ways to validate our feelings. When we feel that the world is in our corner, we search for proof to validate our feeling. Your mind is the master antenna of your life, broadcasting your waves of thought outward into the world. It is not simply a receiver! Taking control of your thoughts means becoming intentional about generating the right images in your mind in order to create the right feelings. When you think about your life, what feelings come up? Go ahead and write out the first 5 sentences about how you feel about your life.

____

____

____

____

____

____

____

____

Do the feelings you have about your life support you becoming the highest version of self? If not, why not? What feelings do you want to experience when you think about your life? When you ask yourself a better question, you get a better answer. The question that should be top of mind for you every morning and every night is…

How do I feel as a completely successful person?

Take a moment to write out your answer to that question. Assume that you are already successful and that all of your dreams have come true. Hold an image of you in the middle of that perfection and then describe how you feel as that perfect version of self, now that it is attained.

____

____

____

____

____

____

____

You get to choose how you feel. Scientifically, the brain has an electrical impulse that creates a chemical and hormonal reaction that results in the "mood" or "feeling" that you have. All of this is the result of two things. What thoughts and physical movement preceded the reaction? Hold yourself in a confident posture. This can be done sitting up, standing up, or even laying down. Picture the image of the perfect you as if you are already there. Hear others telling you amazing things about yourself. Feel what it feels like to have already achieved all of the greatness you desire. Feel into this as often as you can. You can take a 30 second mental break or a 5-minute mental break and achieve this state. The more often you hold the posture of success, the thoughts of success, and the feelings of success inside of you, the easier it is to broadcast the right vibration from the antenna that is your mind.

AROC IN THE HOUSE

You must develop an Anal-Retentive Obsessive-Compulsive drive toward success in order to be the best version of yourself possible. This is not simply a suggestion. It is a requirement! One of the theories that makes a lot of sense to me is the "Theory of Cognitive Dissonance." According to Saul McLeod of Simply Psychology, the theory of cognitive dissonance is when one has conflict between beliefs, attitudes, and actions. When the conflict exists, it creates a psychological discomfort that persists until the person changes what is necessary in order to align the beliefs, attitudes, and actions (McLeod, 2018).

One of the reasons for taking time to feel into the best version of yourself is to generate enough cognitive dissonance related to old habits and behaviors so that it is impossible to act outside of the new belief and feeling. Leon Festinger was the originator of the theory in 1957. His theory was based on observations of a cult that believed the world would end by flooding. The cult members had given up their homes and possessions based on this belief. The fringe members changed their belief to that of being duped out of their savings, left the cult, and pursued life without flooding. The more committed members of the cult chose to realign their beliefs to indicate the flooding had not happened because they were so faithful to the cult. We must either change our behaviors or our beliefs. The choice is ours, but the need for alignment remains consistent.

Think about the image you have of yourself right now and how that image varies from the image of you in your perfect state. When we lay one image over the other in our mind, you see the parts that are not in alignment. You seek a remedy for the alignment issue by changing the behaviors you exhibit or deciding that the perfect you doesn't exist anywhere in time or space. The radically responsible you will have to own the truth that you are making a choice. The choice you are making is to own the truth that you have not acted in the right manner or with the right steps in order to be successful, or that you need to stop believing in your ability to succeed.

When we obsess about success and refuse to even consider the idea that we might not achieve our greatness, we are on the right path! I would never tell you to give up on the image of you living into your greatness. I would tell you, however, that if you choose to not take right action often enough, the people around you will eventually give up on you being successful. Living into a lie will never get you where you want to be. Living with right action, backed by the faith of right beliefs, will make it impossible for you to fail. The actions of success are formulaic. When you are in college, you must attend class, read the materials, do the homework ahead of time, check your work, and do the extra credit when possible. People know this. It is explained in the syllabus. And yet, students still continue to choose to do otherwise.

Sales people know they must have a measured ration of calls/contacts to presentations to deals closed and work completed in order to have the financial success they desire. Yet, you hear sales reps whine all the time about the economy or people simply not doing business. I call bullshit on that one. They did not act according to the formula.

Writers spend time every single day writing. They lay out a book with the chapters and sections within the chapters, or the plot and main storyline, then they begin to write. They write every day and continue to write on a chapter until it is done. If it takes you 30 minutes to write 2 pages of a book and each chapter is going to be 10 pages in length, you need to block off 2.5 hours to write in order to write a chapter in a week.

Leaders spend time every day studying their craft. They connect with their people. They invest time and energy in keeping the vision and mission of the organization in front of their teams. They pay attention to the financials as well as to the emotional queues of their people. They read books on how to lead, go to seminars on how to lead, and set the example of great leadership for their people. They embrace the truth that the example they set is the one that will be followed.

Athletes work out every day. Lebron James is rumored to have spent time twice per day, every day, working on his game, running, exercising, and being dedicated to basketball. Michael Jordan spent hours every day shooting free throws, 3-pointers, jump shots, and lay-ups. He exercised daily. He practiced his dribbling and his ball handling and his dunking. He never quit practicing at any point when he was playing the game he loved.

Stop accepting your own excuses. That shit stinks, and it does not move you forward in life. You have to obsessively pursue the image of you living into your greatness. You must obsess at getting better at your craft. You must build your skill every day. You must go beyond your mere talent and realize that you will only find the success you want when you align the image, the feeling, the belief, the attitude, and the ACTION! Action is the bridge from the unseen to the seen, from the image to the reality. Without action, you will never grow or become better. You will never change!

You know what you need to do in order to be successful. You have likely always known the formula. If you don't know the formula, find a book! Someone has already done what you wish to do or something close enough so that you can learn the formula they used. Make a schedule for yourself that you follow no matter what every single day. Take deliberate action, consistently, and with the kind of drive that would scare the shit out of a drill sergeant. You are the only thing standing between you and the life you desire.

At the end of your life, you will look back and either have your excuses or your results. Which you have is up to you. The walls of our lives are either beautifully painted with deliberate and obsessive actions toward success or plastered with the wallpaper of our excuses. I may not be a true decorator, but I want the success image on my walls.

Take a minute and write out the five steps you will follow every single work day, 5 days a week, without any exception, in order to be successful. Each of us has 5 or fewer things we must do on a daily basis in order to be successful. Put down the action as well as the amount of time you will anal-retentively obsessive-compulsively commit to doing.

Action	Time

If you choose not to do what is necessary, you are not embracing the intrapreneurial or entrepreneurial spirit. You are choosing to act as a failure instead of a success. You are choosing to be less than you are capable of being.

Motivational guru and the father of motivational theory, Abraham Maslow, once said,

"If you intentionally become less than you are capable of being, then I warn you; you will be unhappy for the rest of your life."

I only want you to take the kind of action that leads to cognitive consistency and not to cognitive dissonance. I just can't do life or success or action for you. It is 100% up to you. It is not up to your parents or your friends or your coaches and mentors. It is up to you! What will you choose? Which version of you is going to be the one that wins?

Your ownership mentality is what moves you to act. Your lack of an ownership mentality is what moves you to come up with new and more creative excuses for not being a better version of yourself. Imagine you as a success. Feel yourself to be a success already. Align the actions of a successful person with the image and feeling of success. Do this every day!!!

6 Assume The Position – Leading On Purpose

Experiencing You

I have done thousands of talks on leadership since I began speaking on the subject in 1994. I have asked questions of many of my audiences, exploring what it is that makes a person a leader, and the answers have been interesting. One of the key things you will hear from people is… "Leaders make you feel like you can do more than you believe you can do." It is the feeling that matters greatly in this explanation. A leader is responsible for creating an experience for their people. They are responsible for the emotional, psychological, and often physical well-being of those whom they lead. This is a big responsibility. It is one that most leaders simply ignore in their pursuit of a better P&L statement at the end of the day.

Before you get all pissy that I said money isn't important, hear me out. As a leader, your role is to balance the needs of the organization with the needs of the employees, while ensuring that those clients/customers you serve are getting the highest quality deliverable possible. It isn't just a teeter-totter balancing act. You are balancing in 3, 4, 5 different directions at once.

According to Nilofer Merchant, Stanford lecturer, author, and writer for Harvard Business Review, Drucker's statement that "Culture eats strategy for breakfast every time," is still true today. Merchant indicates that many leaders in business and industry want to know what another company's business strategy is, but they almost never ask about culture or leadership. In the end, it is the culture, the leadership, and the people that will make any company or organization succeed or fail. We see the amount of revenue or the productive output in the metrics our systems measure. That is what makes the discussions about such things easy. However, the people behind the numbers are what make things work. (Merchant, 2011)

Within your leadership position, you can either be wise, intelligent, or both. I had a mentor sit me down right after I started my company in 1999 and tell me that intelligence is the ability to learn a lesson from a mistake and to not make the mistake again; wisdom is the ability to learn a lesson from the mistakes others have made so that I didn't need to ever make those mistakes on my own. Think about that for a minute. How much time does it take to make a mistake and learn from it? It depends on the mistake and your ability to learn, right? When you, as a leader, are willing to admit your mistakes and to grow from them, you set the tone for the people in your organization. You teach them that it is alright to make a mistake as long as you learn from it. When you demonstrate that it isn't alright to make a mistake, you tend to have people who point fingers, blame others, and refuse to accept responsibility for the mistakes made. The culture without accountability reduces productive output and keeps people from growing into their potential.

Without naming any specific airline, I remember speaking with one of the executives to try and understand why their people were so nervous about mistakes. He proudly proclaimed that their CEO had explained to the executives, who had passed the information down the line, that any time a person made a mistake, someone would need to be fired. The CEOs assumption was that this would eliminate mistakes because people would be hyper-focused on ensuring things were done right the first time. The crazy thing is that this actually increased the number of mistakes made, reduced accountability, made people very irritable, and plummetted both customer service and profits. Somehow or another, this airline is still in business and still gaining investors despite their dismal and often non-existent profit margin. That quarter, the airline had posted more than a 10 million dollar loss. What the hell?

Meanwhile, Southwest Airlines had posted yet another profit for the quarter, same quarter, while creating a culture that praised good risk-taking, encouraged joy and laughter, and cared for their people. In talking with several execs from this airline, they explained that the company really cares about them. They "feel" valued and they "feel" like they are a part of something great. That word, feel, is important. In the end, people do what they do because it feels like the right thing to do. The discretionary effort a person gives to a company is based on their feelings related to the company. According to Gallup, a whopping 13% of employees are engaged at work. According to their worldwide (142 country) survey of employees, the results indicated that only 1 in 8 employees is engaged to the point of giving their discretionary effort to improve the bottom-line of the company. The United States and Canada ranked the highest in engagement, but the overall numbers are dismal at best. The study results indicated "low levels of engagement among global workers continue to hinder gains in economic productivity and life quality in much of the world." (Gallup, 2013)

For years, Gallup has studied the impact of leadership on the lives of employees. I have loved the research because it makes my job of explaining the validated need to develop leaders so much stronger. What role do you play in creating engagement? If you are an entrepreneur, you are the king or queen of culture. You are responsible! People work for people, not for companies. Think about a time in your life when you were particularly happy and engaged at work. What was going on? The answers I have gotten with this question keep circling back to feeling in control of one's work and destiny, feeling good about the purpose of the work performed and understanding the purpose, and getting better and better at the work performed. These are the feelings that we, as leaders, must assume responsibility for in the lives of our people. Are you intentionally creating positive emotional experiences? Are you intentionally controlling your own emotions while working with others? Or, are you pitching a fit like a 7 year-old brat and trying to force people to do things? You are responsible for you. And, you are responsible for being intentional when you create an experience of working with/for you. You have to create the right values and beliefs to guide you to success as a leader. You have to demonstrate the right behaviors in order for your people to have something to model. And, guess what? You are responsible for the outcomes as well. Stop blaming others!

Things VARY

I would love to say that I am never an ass-hole at work, but my dad told me that telling lies will land you in a really hot place for all of eternity. So, I will tell you the truth… My name is Jody, and I am not perfect. I make mistakes. I forget to live by my values from time to time. Every now and then, I whine a little. Then I kick my ass back into shape and remember the core of who I am. I want to take you through an exercise that I first introduced in my book, Leadership Evo. This exercise will help you become intentional and purposeful about who you portray yourself as. Let's Dive In!

Values

A person's values are representative of their beliefs in life. In one team-building program I conducted with a rapidly growing tech firm, I had them each list out 5 values that were important to them. I then took the list and combined it into a single list, showing how many times the same words were used to describe important values. I then told them they had to eliminate the complete list down to only 5 values, from around 17. We talked about each of the values, the role each one played in decision-making, and how getting rid of one would be more impactful than another. After an hour of discussion and debate, we got the list down to 5. I then told them they had to give up 1 more value. Which one could we live without? This was tough. They thought they were done at 5 and then had to keep debating. I did this again, and again, and again. Finally, after another 90 minutes of debate, we whittled it down to the 1 value the company would never compromise on. This was an incredibly good feeling for the team to understand the core value that meant everything to them. It is the one they would never compromise on, never accept others compromising on, and would fight for no matter what. That is the value you want to cling to forever! What are your values? Start with a list of 10 and then keep working your way down until you get to the one singular value most important to you, that you would never ever, ever, compromise on, even if some crazy person was threatening your life. You can choose from the list or you can add your own.

My Values…

Check 10	Value	Other Value
☐	Dependability	
☐	Reliability	
☐	Loyalty	
☐	Commitment	
☐	Open-mindedness	
☐	Consistency	
☐	Honesty / Integrity	
☐	Efficiency	
☐	Innovation	
☐	Creativity	
☐	Good Humor	
☐	Compassion	
☐	Adventure	
☐	Motivation	
☐	Positive Attitude	
☐	Optimism	
☐	Passion	
☐	Respect	

☐	Physical Fitness	
☐	Courage	
☐	Personal Growth	
☐	Educating Others	
☐	Perseverance	
☐	Patriotism	
☐	Service To Others	
☐	Environmentalism	
☐	Spiritual Well-Being	
☐	Moving Forward	
☐	Accuracy	
☐	Profitability	

Now that you have gone through and chosen 10, keep crossing out values that are less important until you get down to the one value that matters the most to you. Next, write the value, and then write out at least 5 sentences on why that value is critically important to you and why you would never compromise on it.

My value is: ______________________________

It is important because: ____________________

____

____

____

____

____

____

____

____

Actions

The actions we take are ultimately the measure of where our life ends up. This is why they are so critical in the success equation. The following table has a list of actions you could take. Choose your top 10 actions you believe define you.

Check 10	Action	Other Action
☐	Accomplish	
☐	Achieve	
☐	Analyze	
☐	Attain	
☐	Believe	
☐	Create	

☐	Develop	
☐	Establish	
☐	Exceed	
☐	Fund	
☐	Generate	
☐	Help	
☐	Increase	
☐	Influence	
☐	Justify	
☐	Lead	
☐	Learn	
☐	Manage	
☐	Motivate	
☐	Negotiate	
☐	Organize	
☐	Plan	
☐	Pursue	
☐	Persevere	
☐	Support	
☐	Streamline	
☐	Write	

Follow the same process as before. Once you have chosen your top 10 action words, systematically eliminate one at a time until you narrow it down to the singular action you feel best defines you as a person.

My action is: ______________________________

It is important because: ______________________

____

____

____

____

____

____

____

____

Results

Each of us will be known for a specific set of results. As much as I would love it if I could be known for my awesome intentions, nobody gives a rip. What people care about and how they evaluate a person is ultimately based on the results they achieve. The reality is that others will judge you based on your results, not on your hope for achieving something. In the following chart, write out the top five things you wish to be remembered for achieving. What results will you be known for in this life?

____

____

____

____

____

____

____

____

____

____

If you have written out 5 different results you wish to be remembered for, you can now go back and eliminate one result at a time until you get to the one result you would most regret not being known for. Pick the one you want people to talk about at your funeral, write about in your eulogy, and sit around drinking beer, wishing they could do just like you. That is the result that will matter for the rest of your existence and the rest of your memory.

My result is: ______________________________

It is important because: ____________________

____

____

____

____

____

____

____

____

When you put the statements together, you are able to find the "why" that drives you in life. For example, my three areas were…

Value: Create
Action: Achieve
Result: Highest Potential

I create so that both myself and others can achieve their highest potential.

Once you are able to articulate the thing that drives you, you are more capable of achieving something inspiring in this life. Too many people go through life like the zombies in the movies. They are staring at the 4.7-inch world of their phone and missing out on the greatness inside of them. They end up staying stuck in mediocrity and accepting this as being all life has to offer them. The world is a big-ass place. Turn off your technology from time to time and embrace who you can be in connection to the world around you.

When you focus on being your authentic self, you shed the old skin of conformity and begin truly living. Year after year, I ask people what they want to be when they grow up. Year after year, most people can only talk about being retired, or rich, or something that does not denote having lived a life of purpose. Retired people, those who have lived their life on purpose, can retire with the peace of knowing they have made a positive impact. There is a time to let go of the reigns, but there is also a time to know who you really are.

When I was younger, I was asked to write out what I hoped people would say at my funeral. I wrote about investing in others, being a great father and grandfather, about giving back to the community, and about being the kind of guy that saw the potential in others. After I had written out a beautiful tribute to my dead self, I was then instructed to map out what behaviors I would have had to exhibit each day in order to be remembered in that way. I was then asked to write out what behaviors would keep me from being remembered in that way. That was an incredibly good exercise for me. It forced me to think about life from the perspective of other people around me. I began to watch more of my actions and habits to ensure that others would interpret in me the vision I had for the end of my life. I still strive to live those things to this day. Take a moment and think about your values, actions, and results listed in the previous exercise. As an outside observer watching someone else live those values, actions, and results, what would be your interpretation of their life? Make sure you connect the dots to how you wish to be remembered.

Men In Tights

In wrestling, one of the manliest sports out there, the men wear tights. They get rid of anything that would give their opponent an advantage. They are comfortable with who they are regardless of what their outfits look like. To be comfortable as a leader, you continue to grow and develop. To be comfortable in being successful, you have to get rid of the restraints in your mind and spirit that keep you in the place you have been.

When was the last time you did something that was outside of your comfort zone? For many of the people I coach, they don't want to do things that might make them look cheesy or might attract negative attention from their friends and family. In other words, they are more concerned with appearing cool and broke than they are with actually being successful. As a leader, you will be called on to confront people when you might not want to, learn things that are outside of your standard knowledge set, and live at a higher standard than the people around you. You will be squeezed into the spandex of next level success if, and I do mean if, you are going to truly lead.

Everything you want sits just on the other side of your comfort zone. You are supposed to stretch and pull and change in order to move to the next level. In the video "Leadership Lessons From A Dancing Guy" (Video at: bit.ly/123danceguy), Derek Sivers dissects what it takes to start a movement as a leader. Sometimes you have to be the lone dancing guy who looks goofy and is willing to have others point and stare. Other times, you have to be the first follower, the one who is the actual catalyst for others to follow. The first leader starts the trend, but the first follower starts the movement and makes it okay to go in this new direction.

The bravery it takes for each of the two characters in this real-life drama is immense. I can only imagine what life was like for the Wright brothers in the late 1800's. Wilbur had 4 years of high school and Orville had 3. They did bicycle repair as well as both being retailers, publishers, and writers. They are credited with building and flying the first successful airplane. That is quite an accomplishment, particularly when you think about how others might have looked at them, talked about them, and treated them for doing something that had not yet been done. They were not funded by the government. They were simply driven to lead in this field. Their tenacity to accomplish this task put them as leaders in the aviation industry and inspired first, second, third, and fourth followers to give this new industry their best. Were it not for those brothers leading the way, who knows where the industry would be today?

Even though we would have likely still had airplanes, they might have been built differently, or been delayed by several years, or any number of differences. They had to be willing to step into the spotlight where others might not respect their pursuits. They were not harming anyone around them, but they were changing transportation forever. I always think that if the railroads of that day had thought they were in the transportation business instead of the railroad business, we would have some very different airline names today. They had a comfort zone, though, and stayed in the rail business. Push yourself daily to get outside of your comfort zone like the Wright brothers did, and you will find a world that watches and then follows your lead.

I do realize that there is a great deal of discomfort related to wearing tights, just as there is a great deal of discomfort in being outside of our comfort zones. When we stay stuck in the place where we are comfortable, we don't grow. We stay focused on what we know and what we have experienced, even if it is bad, and we willingly give up our opportunities for greatness.

"One does not discover new land without consenting to lose sight of the shore for a very long time."

--Andre Gide

Let go of the shore. Be your glorious self. Let go of what other people think. Let go of your need for approval from others. You have nothing to prove. You are all that you need!

Sometimes You Go Solo

Leadership begins with one's ability to lead themselves before they lead others. There are five things I would encourage you to focus on in order to master self-leadership.

1. You and only you give meaning to the experiences of your life. Any interaction you have with another person can have an impact. On the other side of that, if you don't give any meaning to an event, then it has no impact on you. That is much easier said than done, but it is possible. What happened in your childhood, at your last job, or wherever else you may have had something difficult in life, those are experiences. The only way that you know if it was bad or good is that you filtered it through your past experiences and chose a label for it. You can allow these experiences to define you, or you can allow them to refine you. Allowing the things you go through to build your potential means finding the lesson in the struggle. I am not

saying this is easy. I am saying it will have an incredible impact on your life, however. Think about some of the things that have been a struggle for you. What is one lesson you could choose from each of those struggles? How did they end up helping you to be a better, stronger, or more prepared for life kind of person? Remember, nothing in this world has meaning except for the meaning I give it. I will choose meanings that support my success!

2. If it will be true, it is up to you. Admittedly this is an adaptation of the old saying, "If it is to be, it is up to me." The point remains the same. You are responsible for yourself. You are not someone else's responsibility. By the time you are an adult, let's say 18 years old, every choice you make is truly your choice. If you make a series of choices that lead you to being broke, those were your choices. If you make a series of choices that lead you to being rich, those were your choices. Stop looking for someone else or something else to blame and start accepting that each choice you make moving forward can shape your life into awesomeness!
3. You are whomever you say you are as long as you believe it. I am a best-selling author. I am not Spiderman®. I can believe the author thing because I can prove that. No matter how hard I have tried, I have never been able to shoot webs or climb buildings without a ladder. When you define yourself, be as specific as possible. Go out of your way to

build a vision of yourself that you write out in the present tense. Read it out loud as often as possible. Spend time feeling what it feels like to be awesome you. Build a vision board with pictures that represent who you are at your most awesome and stare it for a minute or so every day while seeing yourself in that life and feeling the emotional state of that level of success.

4. It's not what's on the inside that the world sees. It's what you do that will define you. Your actions will always speak louder than your words. When you wake up each day and do the things that matter, you move your life forward. If you sleep in too much, take too many naps, don't make your sales calls, or don't deliver what you promised to a client, you will not have success. It is your behavioral habits that will ultimately make you or break you. Think about the 3 to 5 things you need to do every single day in order to be successful. We do so many other things in our day that we often forget to do the things that matter the most. We fall victim to the tyranny of the urgent instead of doing the things that are truly important. Make your list of the most critical things you could do every day in order to move your life towards the vision of success you have built.
5. Stop doing the shit that doesn't work! This may be one of the most important things for your success. I have struggled with this one for quite some time. I do things that are irrelevant toward my success because I feel

guilty. I sometimes help people who don't want to be helped. I create things that only I will ever care about. I speak for free at events where I know there isn't anyone in the audience who can or will ever hire me. Why do I do the shit that doesn't matter? Well, I am pretty sure it is for the same reason you are doing it. You do those things because they are familiar, or you get your ego stroked, or those are the people that look up to you. You do them because you lack the confidence not to do them. These are my reasons, anyway. Step back from your business life and evaluate whether or not the things you are doing are actually moving you forward in life. Anything that is not moving you toward the life you desire, cut it out. To be clear, I am not telling you to get rid of people from your life. I am telling you to protect your time and your knowledge so that they are used to build the life of your dreams. Stop using them to simply get your ego stroked.

Size Matters

The size of your commitment to the cause will be measured regularly. When I was in the middle of a big 'ol struggle to find success, I was offered a six-figure salary with great benefits. I knew I was supposed to be in business for myself, but I hesitated and almost took the job. When things were going great, I was offered a number of distractions that looked like fun and might make me a ton of money. Any of them I tried to get involved with ended up taking away my time and my focus from building my own business. In good times and in bad, you will be tested.

You need to know that you don't have a backup plan. That's right, I did say that you should NOT have a backup plan. I have found that having a backup plan keeps your foot on first base and prevents you from ever stealing second (baseball reference). It keeps you off balance and wavering on your commitment. I remember my grandfather, who was a very strong role model for me, asking me what my backup plan was going to be. He wanted to make sure I had another option when, or if, this business thing didn't work out. I know he meant well. I know my friends who asked the same thing meant well, but it was driving me nuts. I tried to make some things up and think about backup plans at first, but it just seemed to take away my steam and create doubt in my entrepreneurial journey. I found peace when I finally decided that I would either succeed or die trying. This may sound a bit extreme, but it is exactly what is required of us in order to truly find success. Success requires absolute commitment!

The FLOP

Finally Leading On Purpose allows you to get rid of restrictions and be okay with who you are. It positions you to take charge and put in the right efforts instead of sitting around like a whiny idiot, waiting to be saved. There are far too many people going through life as drifters, waiting to see if their circumstances drift them this way or that. It is the drift that kills the flop. Being purposeful in your leadership of self means getting rid of excuses, committing absolutely to a direction, knowing exactly who you are and where you are going, and not allowing yourself to screw around and mess it up.

When we lead ourselves on purpose, we wake up with a plan for the day, check in at noon to ensure we are on track, and review our day at the end of each day. Being purposeful requires us to get rid of the things that hold us back, surround ourselves with people who are going toward the same level of success as we are or who are already there, and to get rid of the tired old excuses we might have used in the past. Our emotional state has a tremendous impact on what we end up doing. This is why being purposeful and choosing our emotions will matter as well.

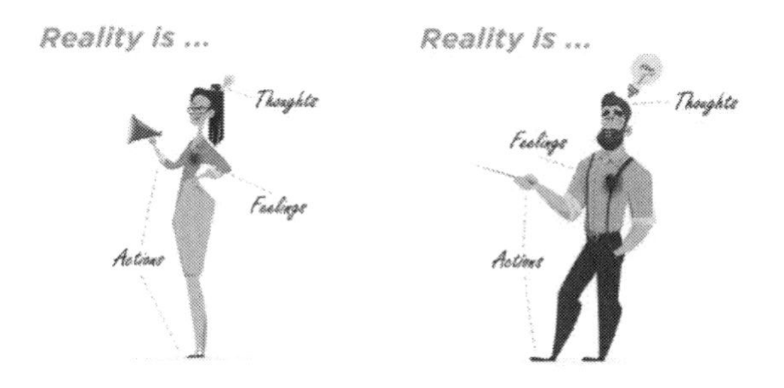

First thing in the morning, establish your thoughts for the day and hold body posture like you are supremely confident. Your body posture, or physiology, will stimulate your emotional state. Have your time planned out in chunks with the most important things being done first. You must focus on the things that create success before you focus on the things that are simply there in your day. Keep a log of the actions you are taking and whether or not they are moving you toward your objectives. If they are moving you forward, keep them. If they are not, dump them. At the end of each day, review your actions taken during the day and evaluate your progress. Then, plan out your next day to ensure you stay on track. Finally, as you drift off to sleep, hold a vision or image of what your life is like when it is completely successful and feel into that success. Hold the positive feeling as you drift off to sleep. This moves the reality of your success into your subconscious mind. You must align your thoughts, feelings, and actions in order to be successful. If your feelings are off, the whole thing is thrown off. Stay focused on this routine and you will be amazed at what you accomplish.

Now, go Get Shit Done! #gsd

7 Start A C.U.L.T.-ure

"Culture eats strategy for breakfast every day."
--Peter Drucker

According to Psychology Today, there are specific reasons as to why people are engaged or disengaged in the workplace. The smaller the business, the more critical it is to have high engagement with your team. When you have 3,000 employees and 300 or so of them are disengaged and not really accomplishing anything, this hurts less than if you have 5 employees and 1 is disengaged. David DiSalvo goes on to say that we draw on the things from our childhood that excited us. Those who imagined constructing great buildings are more passionate about architecture and construction. Those who loved to write or tell stories would be more passionate about writing books, developing narratives, and sharing the story of the business (DiSalvo, 2012).

Each of us has a reason we do the things we do. When we seek out places to go to work, we often imagine what the values of the organization will be, what their culture will be like, and what we will feel as we work there. There will be a challenge that we feel is perfect for us to resolve. It is this challenge that has likely driven our lives up to that point and will continue to do so as we move forward. In the end, our objective must be to create passionate people who share values and a vision for the future. When we are able to create that pathway that fuels their spirits and inspires action, we are on the path to incredible success.

For years, I have described how I wanted the best of the best on my team and I wanted fewer people. I think about the special forces teams in the military. I think about the sniper who can sit a thousand yards away and win a fight without ever being seen. I am not saying anything negative about the rest of the military personnel. I am simply saying that I strive to have the very best of the very best on my team. The military invests quite a bit more in the training and preparation of the special forces. The special forces individual invests a great deal more energy and self-sacrifice than other positions in the military as well. Those are the people who build the foundation of our cultures. We need the people who are incredibly passionate, perhaps to a super-human level of intensity, in order to change the world.

Several of the team members I have had over the years worked so many hours that I had to remind them to take time off. It was not an expectation I had of them. I did set an example of being passionate about my work and being willing to put in the hours to find success, but I never asked them to do the same. They took it upon themselves to be that driven because the mission and vision of our company became their mission and vision as well. The first key piece of your success is to put your mission, values, vision, and company personality in the spotlight in order to make sure you are on the right track.

Your cult-ure will either make you or break you. Culture can be described as the personality of an organization. Think about the people that you really can't stand in this world. Is it their hair that drives you crazy? That isn't likely. It is typically the personality of the person that we can't stand. Their personality determines their beliefs, thoughts, actions, and results. When we can't stand the way a person acts, we are actually saying we can't stand the personality of the person. The same thing is true of the businesses we work for, build, or interact with. If we can't stand a company, it is because it has a bad culture as compared to our expectation of cultural greatness.

Culture

Here are the 7 things that must be addressed in order for a culture to be developed into its highest potential.

Company values – The values of a company are the beliefs about the world from the people running the business. Values are how we filter our world. If one of our values is fun, we find that we ask ourselves whether or not a direction will bring fun to our team before we embark on that journey. Typically, the values of the people in charge will become the values of the organization. This is why it is so critical to have a strong screening process, particularly for the people who will have any level of authority in your business.

Company Norms – Norms are the expectations we would have for the behaviors of people within an organization. The manner in which people interact with one another, the model for doing business, and the expected standards for those interactions work together to make up the company norms. When we are not intentional about the norms and expectations we have of our people, we are being intentional about NOT owning the outcomes of our organizational success.

Leadership Style – We often expect others to judge us as leaders based on our best intentions. That isn't how the world works, though. Leadership style is the behavioral representation of how leaders view their employees at all levels. If we were judged based on our intentions, there would be a lot of husbands out there being praised for simply intending to buy their wives flowers. It is what we do that matters more than what we intended to do. How a leader behaves represents the thoughts they have about their team. Their thoughts represent their beliefs about the team. Step back from your role as a leader and determine how you wish to see your people. What are the labels that build people's potential? Those are the beliefs you need as a great leader.

Ethical Standards – One's ethical standards reveal their model for decision-making in any given situation. If you live by the standard that not telling the truth is never an option, then even when it would be difficult to open up and tell the truth, you do it. Telling a lie would be inconceivable to you. In my book Yay! I'm A Supervisor! Now What!?, I outline that people see ethics as Absolute, Legalistic, Situational, or Optional. I believe most people know the difference between right and wrong. The difference maker in being seen as ethical is in choosing right as a norm for decision-making instead of just choosing profits regardless of right or wrong.

Communication – The vast majority of the issues I have dealt with over the last couple of decades of consulting and coaching relate to poor communication. When communication goes wrong, people feel undervalued and unappreciated. When communication goes wrong, people don't know what is expected of them. There are two sides to communication in business. First, we must focus on being great listeners with our team. I talk about the 4 steps to being a great listener in both Yay! I'm A Supervisor! and in Leadership Evo (http://bit.ly/jodyholland). When we listen, people feel connected with us, appreciated, valued, and inspired to give more of what they have to offer. The second side of communication relates to setting clear expectations. When we set an expectation, it must describe what we expect, when we expect it by, and how we will measure its success. If we will manage those two key components of communicating, many of the business problems we experience will simply go away.

Why We Are Here – This is a very big deal. We look at our world in business and often think we are here only to make a great profit. Money cannot be the primary goal. Cultures deteriorate very quickly when money is the primary driver for business. When money is the goal, ethics almost certainly slip. There must be a bigger reason for the existence of a business. There must be a "why" that inspires action from your teams. Simon Sinek discusses how most companies talk about what they do and many of them even talk about how they do what they do. Very few companies even know or discuss why they are doing what they do. When we can answer the why with a reason that builds our world, our employees get excited. The why answer is the pathway to tapping into the emotional triggers of a person. In the end, we are all feeling, or emotional creatures, not logical creatures. My why for being in business is… I am here to find and develop the potential of my clients so they can find greater success, satisfaction, and peace. The simple version of how to develop your why statement would be…. My company is here to _________________ so that _________________.
When you can fill in those two blanks and embrace the idea of your why statement guiding your decisions at work, you have found your reason for succeeding. To quote Simon Sinek, "Always start with why."

Build People Up – We live in a world now where people work for people, not for companies. The greatest asset any company has is its people. You can have a mediocre idea and great people and you will win. Or, you can have a great idea with mediocre people, and you will lose. A great culture embraces the value of the people who run the show. At every level, your people are important. Each person has value, and each position is critical. When you see the value of each person in each position within the company, you invest time and energy in them. This is a daily leadership choice. If we are choosing to use people as pawns in a game, or if we are choosing to embrace the value and importance of each person, we are simply making a choice. What will your choice be?

Understanding

To understand a company is to understand its story. When we are thinking about who we wish to be known as, we must address the stories that others will both imagine and share about our organization. Whether you are a business that is owned, operated, managed, and run by only you, or if you are a business that has thousands of employees, your story matters. In working with businesses on growth, I have often reminded the founder to tell the story of why and how the company came to be. This story outlines the values of the organization, the original desire to create something great in the market or to change the marketplace at a fundamental level. It is the inspiration that lets people know why they should be excited to be a part of the organization. There are seven areas that one should address in telling a great story.

The Key Elements of Your Story – Every great story has a reason for being told. "So, there we were thinking, that would make us rich…" is a horrible start to a story. Don't get me wrong, I really like the end result of making money. However, your story has to be about something bigger than money. It has to be about making a splash in the market, putting a ding in the universe, bringing fundamental and needed change to the world, etc. Your story has to be built on a greater purpose. Go back to your why statement. That is the basis for the story you are telling in the market. You are here to _______________ so that _______________. This inspires you because _______________. You are excited about this story/journey because _______________. You are excited about your team being a part of it because _______________.

The Conflict In The Story – Once you have outlined the key elements of your story, you need to carefully outline the conflict in the story. All great movies have both a conflict and a resolution. If you have no conflict, there is very little of interest to talk about. Sometimes the conflict is that other organizations are taking advantage of people in this space and you are fighting against that abuse. The conflict might be fighting against elderly people having to age without dignity and grace because of a lack of quality providers in long-term care. The conflict might be fighting against an old way of doing things that keeps the world stuck. Whatever it is you are fighting against, be ready to fight. Be ready to know that you are in a battle to make the world a better place with the product or service you are offering. Some of the most passionate people I have seen are those in MLM (multi-level marketing) companies. Quite often, they are fighting against having a traditional job that keeps people stuck, away from their families, and restricted by someone else's determination of their worth. This is a noble battle, and it inspires people to jump on board even if they have never sold anything or recruited anyone before in their life.

When our story has a strong enough and important enough conflict, we inspire others to want to be a part of where we are going. Conflict is powerful! What injustice do you stand against? I began training because I had seen some incredibly bad trainers who were arrogant and really only cared about reading their beautiful PowerPoint to you. As someone who develops the potential in others so they can be a positive force in all they do, I had seen lots of trainers whose only conflict they were raging against was that of getting more money out of companies. What is it that you cannot stand that relates to your industry? What would you fight against for the rest of your life? Knowing what gets you fired up will often get the people who work for you fired up as well. Most people are seeking direction for the battle. Very few people are waking up and raging against something without first being pointed in a direction by a leader. You are that leader!!! Pick your conflict and demonstrate a passion that fires people up to want to be on your team.

The Hero Of The Story – Every story requires a hero. It requires a person or a group who stands in the face of injustice, arms locked, ready to make the world a better, safer, more inspiring place to be. Batman raged against the criminal underworld of Gotham. Spiderman stood and swung against the bad guys in his neighborhood. I stand firmly against people letting their potential go to waste. While I would love to be Spiderman and solve conflict through acrobatics, flying webs, and kick-ass fight scenes, I never found that perfect spider bite to transform me. Instead I have to transform myself into the hero of the story. As a side note, I do realize we have talked about being a caring respecter instead of a hero, but in a story, people want to know who it is that plans to save the day. They want to know who to look to in order for their problem, conflict, or challenge to be resolved. I am not encouraging you to look at others and think they are incapable of solving a problem. Rather, I am encouraging you to see their potential while living into the storyline of having answers that make their potential greater.

Heroes know their purpose, show their passion for their purpose by taking specific action, and live each day as someone who stands both for a cause and against a conflict. In the story of your company or brand, you must play the part of the one who is there to save the day. I am a hero in the training and coaching arena. This is because I stand against bad training, those who have no real purpose other than being in the business, and training or coaching that does not produce positive change. I know why I am here. I have cultivated my talents in this field. I invest regularly in myself and in my potential so that I have more and more to offer. Even comic-book heroes trained for their journey. Peter Parker didn't just wait for trouble, he prepared to fight against it as the hero he was meant to be. Can you see yourself as a hero? Can you find the passion needed to make the world a better place in the industry you serve? You will have to in order for others to see you as the hero. People see us how we see us.

Your G.P.S. Guides You – Your goals, plans, and strategies will guide you as the hero of your story. Once you have chosen the thing you are fighting against and can clearly see yourself as a hero in the fight, you have to have goals, plans, and strategies in order to win. When I really started becoming successful at writing books, coaching people, and training teams, it was because I set a goal to help a certain number of people in a year. I became clear about my role within the conflict and then created a plan for how I was going to help, what I was going to offer, and why I was doing what I was doing. My strategy became one of helping others in settings where I could demonstrate value so that the participants in these programs would want to hire me to demonstrate more value. I have worked with chambers of commerce, trade associations, and community leadership groups in order to tell my story and invite others to bring me in as a part of their story.

Whether it is telling your story on social media, telling it as a speaker in groups of people who can and likely will buy from you (my strategy), or putting out videos and content that challenge people to become a part of your story (Gary V's strategy), the plan is the same. You must plan to tell your story in a way that stimulates a positive response from others. People buy Apple products because they want to be part of the storyline. Apple stands against the status quo in the industries they serve. They do this by creating products that fundamentally change the way an industry operates. Zappos stands against retail shoe locations, big box stores, and the inconvenience of going to the store and dealing with unhappy employees. They provide free shipping both directions on shoes you buy as well as shoes you return. They want you to see and feel and try on the shoes in your own home. Warby Parker stands against overpriced glasses and optometrist's offices that rip people off with frames they have marked up several hundred percent. They accomplish this through the strategy of allowing you to get up to 5 frames sent to you at your house so you can walk around the house, look in the mirror, and feel what a frame would feel like. People often end up buying multiple frames from them because they are more affordable and have great service. Your story is filled with the actions you have taken to demonstrate your values and beliefs as an organization. You as an entrepreneur have to know why you are here and develop the skills to articulate that reasoning. Strategy matters because it is the action behind your story!

Your Solution Is Your Connection – People want a solution to whatever challenge they are facing. I have never gone to the doctor because I like them to run tests on me. I have never thought… "I would love it if someone took some of my blood today and didn't give it back or even use it for someone else." That doesn't happen. By the same measure, nobody is going to buy your product or your service just because. That isn't what they are looking for. Anyone making a purchase wants to achieve an end result. As an example, if you have clothes you wear and get dirty, you want to purchase a washing machine, so you have clean clothes to wear. It is not the act of washing that seems to really excite people. It is the act of wearing clean clothes that excites them. Driving a car is not about getting you from point A to point B. If that were the case, we would each purchase the minimum amount of vehicle possible. A person's car becomes their statement. Some buy great gas mileage to demonstrate their conservative nature and their desire to save the planet. Some buy large vehicles to demonstrate their ability to haul stuff or to show off their youth sports hauling and child transport proficiencies. I drive a luxury sports car to demonstrate that I am successful and that clients can trust that plenty of other clients have already trusted me. Whatever your story is that you are trying to get across to others, rest assured that you have a story.

One of the oldest lessons in sales is that of the quarter-inch drill bit. Every year, millions of quarter inch drill bits are sold without one single person actually wanting to buy a quarter inch drill bit. What people want is a quarter inch hole and that is achieved only if they first purchase a quarter inch drill bit. This solution-based selling works incredibly well because it positions you as a partner in the sales process. As a leader, you are constantly influencing others. Influencing and selling are brothers from the same mother. Consider the truth of your success to be in direct correlation to your ability to discover the end result another person desires plus your ability to demonstrate that you or your company can build a bridge to that end result with what you offer.

In my book My Judo Life, Cody Stephenson is the main character and he gets downsized. He had an appointment in the afternoon after being let go in the morning. He decided to go to the appointment despite not have a job anymore. When he sits down in front of the executive he is there to see, the exec asks him what he is selling. Cody replies, "nothing." He goes on to ask what is important to the exec and his team. In the conversation, he begins to use good problem solving to understand the end result desired by that particular exec. After a great conversation and a little white-board session, he discovers the solution desired and builds a plan to get to the solution. The executive was inspired by the process and asks Cody to help his team do the same thing and wants him to provide the solution they discussed. The fundamental shift that happened when Cody focused on helping the exec find the right solutions for him and his team was that the executive decided he wanted to buy from Cody (Holland, 2015). When we provide solutions instead of selling products and services, we are seen as a partner in the process instead of a salesperson. I don't know anyone who wants to be sold. I know countless numbers of people that like to buy, though! Provide solutions instead of selling, and you become the best partner the business has ever met!

Celebration Is A Partnership – Think about some of the things organizations do to celebrate a victory for a customer or client. I see real estate agents taking pictures of their customers in front of their new house and then posting how joyous they are that they were able to help another family realize their dream of the perfect home. In this scenario, the real estate agent is saying they are happy for the family and also saying they are happy they had a hand in finding the perfect home for them. This connection is what gets other people to think… "I want to be as happy as a family in a new home, so I better get ahold of that real estate agent." Car salespeople will take pictures of a customer holding the keys to their brand-new ride. They also often have the customer say what they loved about the experience, the new ride, or simply how they felt in that moment. Each of us is seeking the achievement of positive emotional experiences and the avoidance of negative emotional experiences. When we see another person achieving what we wish to achieve, we put ourselves in the place of the customer and think about what it would be like as us in the picture. In my case, I am helping organizations live into their mission and achieve at higher levels through their people. When I am successful in doing my job, they are more successful in doing their jobs. I celebrate the advancement of their success… because I provided the right tools and skills to achieve at that higher level.

When a person celebrates as a part of your story, they are celebrating your company. Their entire objective was to find the solution that you helped guide them toward. They do the work, but they need you to build the road to that definition of success, that destination. They celebrate because they have achieved something of greatness. They also celebrate you because you helped to guide them into that greatness. One of the tactics I use to be a celebration partner with my clients is to write papers about the client and their journey with the services I am providing. I know that many of the clients I work with are seeking ways to live into their mission while achieving more stable financial footing. To date, no client has asked me to help them avoid their mission or make less money in the process. A white paper is a description of the process, people involved, and actions taken to find success using the systems or tools I provide. By describing the process followed and the results the client received by participating in the process, I am celebrating their success while reminding them that I was a catalyst for their greater success. I don't take credit for the success. Instead, I celebrate that in our partnership we were able to achieve the level of success desired.

When you celebrate your client, you celebrate your role in the story of that client. If you forget to include yourself in the story, you have not lived into the partnership of celebration that was fully intended. You have also given up the best opportunity you had to create a lasting emotional connection as well as the perfect positioning for you and your company. Write yourself into the story because you have been an integral part of the story. Honor your work by sharing the credit. Do not dishonor the client by taking the credit, though. Your organization and effort in partnership with the client are how you achieved success. Never downplay that!

Leadership

You can lead a horse to water, but you can't make him drink. I remember hearing my grandfather say this multiple times when I was young. As a kid, I just assumed he was saying that horses were just dumbasses. In hindsight, he wasn't talking about horses at all. He was talking about the people he had working for him. Did I mention that I spent a little time working for my grandfather? Anyway, the point of the statement is to get people to realize that a leaders' job is to set up a scenario for success. A leader can't do the work for the person. They can lead the way, but they can't be the way all on their own. If you have ever worked with horses and tried to get a horse to do what you wanted it to do, you know the frustration that comes from trying to "make" a horse act in a certain way. The frustration relates to trying to push or prod the animal into submission. Horses are both conditioned leaders and great followers. When you are trying to get a horse to go into the barn to saddle him/her, you don't yell at the horse. You also don't get behind the horse and push. That leads to visits to the doctor, or at least to the chiropractor. You simply hold the reigns in your hand and lead the horse into the barn.

People are not that drastically different from any of the other species of followers and leaders. Being a leader is about defining what your characteristics are and then reverse engineering the behaviors that would fit best to make those characteristics unmistakable. If a person says that they are a leader with integrity, how do we know? It is solely based on the things the leader does, not on what they say they are going to do. Consider this, when we are building a cult-ure within our organization, there are characteristics of leadership that make this flow the most smoothly.

The best of the best in leading great cultures have the following as a part of who they are. They have a foundation of understanding, a core set of beliefs focused on the potential and beauty of their people, and the behaviors to make those things visible.

Foundation

Let's start with the foundation of understanding. To have this understanding, one must have experienced life at multiple levels within an organization. Over the last couple of decades of doing leadership and organizational development for companies, the leaders who are the most engaging have been the ones that truly understand the business at each level. Think about the show Undercover Boss, every time the boss interacts as an employee to understand the struggles at a different level, he or she comes out thinking, "How the hell do my people do this?" and wanting to fix things. I have yet to see an episode where the boss thought everything was all good and they didn't need to invest anymore in their people or change anything. It is easy to forget what people go through when you remove yourself from connection to those people. I am not saying a person cannot succeed as a leader if they did not work their way up from the bottom in an organization. I am saying, however, that it is incredibly difficult for a person to understand their people if they stepped straight into a leadership role and never really had a job where they struggled. Even Charles Schwab started with Andrew Carnegie's railroad empire as just another guy on the line driving railroad spikes with a sledge-hammer. The difference between a person who moves up and a person who stays driving spikes is their desire to understand all levels of the business. This is just as true for people who stay at the top as those who stay at the bottom. Seeking to understand what each employee is going through makes a huge difference in the way those employees feel. It also reduces the amount of griping or excuse-making when your employees know that you have actually done their job in the past.

Beliefs

The second piece to the leadership puzzle relates to what people believe about their employees. I have seen leaders on both sides of the equation with this. Some leaders see the beauty and possibility in their people, and others see only the cost and struggle in them. What a person sees has little to do with what is right in front of them and more to do with what is inside of them. Our minds are incredibly powerful. They are so powerful that our beliefs will determine whether or not other people are good at their job, or if we are going to seek out what is wrong so intensely that we keep them from success.

John Lubbock said, "What we do see depends mainly on what we look for. ... In the same field the farmer will notice the crop, the geologists the fossils, botanists the flowers, artists the colouring, sportsmen the cover for the game. Though we may all look at the same things, it does not all follow that we should see them."

— John Lubbock, The Beauties of Nature and the Wonders of the World We Live In

I would encourage you to make a list of the attributes you would like to see in your people. Try to keep it to the top 5 things you could see in them for them to be incredible. Then, spend a few moments each day visualizing your people living fully into that vision.

What makes my employees incredible is…

____

____

____

____

____

Training

What is more expensive than hiring a person, investing time and money in training them, and then having them leave? The answer is: hiring a person and not investing time and money in training them, and then having them stay! Training is an ongoing process. Each level of employment requires a new set of skills. To go from an employee to a supervisor requires that you develop the skills of a supervisor. The skills I recommend and teach to my client companies are:

- Business 101 – Understanding the basics of self-management, hiring and firing, authority, safety at work, and leveraging talent
- Learn-2-Lead – An in-depth look at the 12 skills of a great leader. These skills help anyone in charge to ensure work gets done properly at all levels in the organization. It helps the leader to motivate, coach, correct, and inspire greatness in their teams.
- Lead-2-Inspire – To truly lead, one must master strategy, style, culture, vision, and execution. To inspire greatness in another person is to embrace their free will while seeking out their greatness.
- Team Building – Tapping into the model of engagement that leads teams to connect at a deeper level and overcome the dysfunctions that prevent them from achieving their full potential

- Project-Management and Problem Solving – Understanding how to get a handle on keeping projects, tasks, and people on track, as well as solving problems that will inevitably arise.
- Sales and Service Mastery – Using relational and connection skills coupled with effective strategies to expand the outreach of an organization

The Leadership Skills I teach go in-depth and are titled *Learn-2-Lead* and *Lead-2-Inspire*. There are 12 topics in the *Learn-2-Lead*, 1-year series. The second 1-year series is *Lead-2-Inspire*. Most companies I work with also have customized coaching and training programs beyond that. The point is that there really isn't an end to what a person can and should learn. When we are continuously focused on developing the potential of our people, we are ALWAYS in training and development mode. The same is true for us! We should never stop learning.

Radical Responsibility – The Glue That Keeps The Cult-ure Going

If I am radically responsible for myself, then I do not blame others. I simply act in the right direction and do not blame anyone or anything for my choices. I am in control of my mind, my emotions, my actions, and my outcomes. I am who I am and where I am because I have chosen to be here. Say it with me! I am who I am and where I am because I have chosen to be here. You don't accept any of those bullshit excuses even from yourself for why your culture isn't better. I have seen a great culture in a porta-potty business and a horrible culture in a bank. I have seen a great culture in a bank and a bad one in an auto-body shop. Great cultures have nothing to do with the industry. Instead, they have everything to do with you, the leader, accepting radical responsibility for creating that great culture. So, what's it going to be? Are you radically responsible or simply an excuse maker?

Now is your time to step up and own responsibility for making your business incredible. Stop using the excuse that you would have a great culture if you were rich like Google or one of the other tech firms. I would argue that their culture was great before they were rich. Now, they are rich because they had a great culture. How you treat your people will determine how your people treat your customer, which will determine how your customer treats your bottom-line. There are no excuses; there are only choices.

8 W.T.F. – Write The Future

I'm Pregnant

The wonderful thing about the future is that it already exists in possibility. When we begin to think about the future and all of the things in our vision, our minds begin to immediately run scenarios of potential outcomes. I think back to when my wife and I started getting serious in our relationship. For me, that was about 1 date in. For her, it was several months into the relationship. Once we both saw each other as the one to spend our lives with, the pictures of the future began to come into focus. We would take walks through neighborhoods and look at the houses, the yards, the families, and the dreams that were represented in those things. It was the idea of being together with those things that pulled us toward the future. We began to lay out dreams of what life would be like for us 5 or 10 or even 20 years down the road. Before my wife, I don't remember being able to see anything in the future. Although we have had our troubles, the same as most couples, she has pushed me to be that better version of myself that has always existed.

Our conscious minds represent the male portion of the mind. Our subconscious minds represent the female portion of the mind. The conscious mind pushes thoughts and ideas into the subconscious, but it is the subconscious that does the real work. What you walk around telling yourself is critically important for this very reason. If you are impregnating your subconscious with thoughts of hope and joy and success and possibility, your subconscious will bring those things to pass. If you are impregnating your subconscious with weakness and despair and doubt, your subconscious will bring those things to pass. Borrowing from Jungian psychology, the two sides of our thought processes come together to form the one individual. Jung referred to this collaboration as individuation. When our conscious mind pushes ideas, the subconscious goes about filtering our experience of the world in the field of potential in order to bring those things into awareness.

We were created to create. Our sole purpose for existence on this earth is to bring creation to life. We create by believing in ourselves, in the field of possibility, and in our connection between the two halves of our consciousness. I think back to the scene in "My Big Fat Greek Wedding," where the bride's mother (Maria Tokalos) looks at her and says, "the man may be the head of the household, but the woman is the neck; and it can turn the head any way she wants." That is the way of the subconscious. It is the neck, and it is continuously turning the component of observation to catch the things that matter the most, based on how it was programmed.

The aspect of impregnating an idea is either done on purpose or it is purposely done by accident. I know that is a bit confusing, so let me clarify. When we become what the world around us tells us to be, we are accidently becoming a person. Nevertheless, we are still becoming what we allow ourselves to be programmed to become. When we are purposeful about taking charge of our lives, we put specific things into our minds. We intentionally create an image of ourselves in our conscious awareness and push that image into our subconscious being. Conscious mind is awareness. It is observable. It is on purpose. It is logic. The subconscious mind is being. It is feeling. It is emotion. It is the essence of living. Your job in writing the future is to take control of what you pass from conscious awareness into subconscious being. You need a strategy in order to make that happen.

When we impregnate an idea into our minds, we begin to notice things that might not have been noticeable before. The R.A.S. (reticular activating system) is what is responsible for that noticing. This is a tool of the subconscious that allows us to take in maximum input without flooding the conscious mind and shutting it down. There are two times that the R.A.S. is most susceptible to programming inputs. That is within the first few minutes of waking up and within the last few minutes of being awake. Most of the people I have interacted with wonder why they have more trouble sleeping as they get older. My theory is that we hold onto more stress as we age and feel more compelled to figure things out. We lay down at night, thinking about the day, about what went right and what went wrong, and wondering how we are going to make things better tomorrow. When we lie down with our anger and our stress, we overload our conscious mind and send signals to the subconscious that we are in need of assistance. The conscious mind is telling the subconscious that it cannot figure things out, that it is in struggle. Therefore, the subconscious spends its time trying to find ways to justify the struggle and stress it was told represent us. It creates struggle and stress!

At night, create an image of everything going perfectly in all aspects of your life. Hold the image only long enough to generate a feeling that all is perfect. I ask myself the question, "what would I feel like if this image were true?" The reality of the image is not relevant. We only need the image long enough to generate the feeling. Once the feeling is in place, hold the feeling as you drift off to sleep. When you wake, start the day with a grateful heart. I do two things each morning as I rise. First, I list off the things I am grateful for. Second, I state my I AM statements out loud. *I am the most sought-after trainer in the United States. I am a best-selling author. I am honored by my family and my community.* I do realize that some I AM statements can sound a bit arrogant and that's okay. The reality of these statements is that they are lines of programming code. They are impregnating the subconscious and guiding it to do its incredible work. Be very careful what you put into the subconscious. It will only create based on the input it is given.

You will be amazed at two aspects of what you experience when you begin doing this. First, you will be amazed at the amount of fighting that your own mind might do to keep you where you are. Second, you will be even more amazed at the growth and success that happen in your life as a result of sticking with it. When you get serious about connecting with the source energy that is a part of your very being, you unlock the greatness that has always been inside of you. You see the potential that has always been right there, waiting to be released into this world. In utero, a female baby already has the eggs that will grow and develop. They already have the potential of the next generation inside of them before they are even born. I get that change can be scary and even intimidating, but life is just like that. Birthing a new version of yourself can be messy and scary and nerve-racking. This creation thing is what sets you apart from those who will simply allow the world around them to create on their behalf. For me, I am choosing to be the creator of my own story. Are you?

Was That Good For You?

Life is a series of choices made by each of us with the intent of protecting us from something bad. We go to a specific school because it is safe and funded and secure. We marry the person we marry because others will approve. We do the things we do in order to stay in a good place. Too often we are going through life trying to arrive as safe as possible at death. One of my friends described that he wants people to look at his open casket and say, "Geez, that guy must have really lived!" When we make our way through life and set out to write our own futures, we need to be, no we must be willing to take the kind of risks that push us outside of our comfort zones.

Most people have a zone in which they operate. They don't want things to get too good because it would freak them out. They don't want things to get too bad because that would also freak them out. They want things to stay in that mediocre, yet somewhat unsatisfying range. That's right. I did say it was unsatisfying. Think about it for a minute. Do you gather around the person who starts their story with, "so there we were being safe and following all of the rules," or do you huddle close to the person who says, "I knew there was danger, but I also knew I had to see if it was possible?" I am hanging with Dangerous Dave, not Safety Steve. I am not encouraging you to take uncalculated risk. Instead, I am commissioning you to have the kinds of dreams and plans that scare the crap out of you, at least a little. If it doesn't scare you at least a little, why the hell are you doing it?

Crash happens. When we begin to push ourselves to be more, do more, and have more, we often run into that brick wall of "what the hell was I thinking?" When we begin to rise above the image we have of ourselves, our subconscious minds grab our floating successful selves by the ankles and body slams us back into reality. It reminds of who we are because it reminds us of who we programmed ourselves to be. The reason I discussed impregnating a new image of yourself before discussing the crash is so that you would understand the importance of the right accepted self-image. Let's say you have a possible range of success that ranges from 0 to 100. Your normal might be in the 40 to 60 range. About the time you reach 65 or 70, your mind begins to tell you that the other shoe is about to drop. Your family is going to hate you for outdoing them. Your kids will turn out to be spoiled brats. You aren't worthy of this level of success. It makes up all kinds of crazy thoughts just to bring you back. What normally happens is you crash down below your comfort zone because of the subconscious and very negative attacks you are making on you. Once you are below the comfort zone, you slowly but surely begin your correction into the zone. You move up and down between 40 and 60, happily occupying your space of mediocrity, even though you were meant for greatness.

The key to getting out of the zone is to move yourself up a few notches at a time. A complete overhaul generally results in an equivalent or greater crash. You then have to course correct to even get back up to the zone. I do realize that there are a number of self-help geniuses out there who tell you that you can change in an instant. I have even seen people do that. Most people, however, need a lifestyle change, not a radical diet change to become the person they were meant to be. Lifestyle changes are incremental. They are one step at a time in the right direction. When you focus on seeing yourself at one level up from where you are right now, your mind more easily accepts that as possible and potential. When you visualize yourself as the greatest person in the world even though you have never demonstrated it, your mind calls B.S. on you. You crash hard and then get pissed off at the asshole who made you try that crap in the first place. Stay focused on the climb. Stay focused on moving up 5 points at a time so that your comfort zone moves to a 45 to 65 range and then a 50 to 70 range and so on. You can achieve the life that you can accept as real.

How good can you stand it? The amazing thing about this comfort zone is that when you get close to the 80 to 100 range, a whole new zone comes into view. The world continues to expand and expand, allowing you to grow and achieve and succeed without any ceiling to stop you. The only stop is the answer to the question… how good can you stand it? That is the question you must be able to answer at the next level each and every time. Take just a minute and write out how good you could stand it if your world changed today. Be honest about what you would accept and what you would not accept relating to your rise to greatness.

____

____

____

____

____

____

____

Ain't Nobody Got Time For That

Our ability to procrastinate is often the very thing that keeps us from living the life we desire and running the kind of company we want to run. One of the key characteristics of a successful person is their ability to kill the urge for instant gratification and choose directed action over undirected inaction. I heard Tim Urban's TED talk on procrastination a couple of years ago. He tells the story of how the mind of a procrastinator is, perhaps, different than the mind of a non-procrastinator. He suggests that a procrastinator's mind has an instant gratification monkey in it that distracts the captain of the ship and turns the ship towards fun. He calls the fun zone that provides no inherent value, the "dark playground." He has a masterful way of explaining what happens in our minds using a fun anecdote. I believe that millions of people in the U.S. alone can relate to his description of the instant gratification monkey. He even talks about how the monkey is only afraid of the panic monster. This monster comes out when things are on the verge of being too late to complete. It scares the monkey away and puts the captain back at the wheel in hopes of getting the ship back on track.

In my opinion, learning to overcome that crazy desire for instant gratification is a battle most people fight. Whether you are endeavoring to write a book, get six-pack abs, sell a product or service, or start a business, that desire to do the easier thing seems to be ever present. Many times, people don't even realize what is going on in their minds as this happens. When you have a deadline imposed by someone else, you know that you are supposed to get things done within that window of time. When there is no deadline, things get more complicated. I think that this one thing is what keeps the best separated from the rest. I am not sure I can even count the number of talented people who have chosen procrastination over success, just in my direct experience. It seems to be more common than focus in this world.

Get perspective. We often look at the task at hand and think it is overwhelming or simply too much. We think of it as something that might kill us. In other words, we blow shit out of proportion. This all or nothing thinking often keeps people from building any kind of real momentum in their minds. Stop worrying about what others might think and simply write. Stop wondering if you will ever be able to complete the task and just act. When we narrow our focus down to the thing we CAN do right now, we gain the perspective of self-control. Being in control of our next move is really all that we have. Don't worry about 5 moves out. Just worry about the next move you are going to make. Your business model, your strategy, your long-term success should be a part of your plan, but you can only control what happens next, not what happens next year.

Know your why. The is a reason you are launching the business, writing the book, painting the painting, finding your fortune, or whatever other endeavor you are embarking on. What is it? Why are you doing what you are doing? I remember thinking as a new entrepreneur, "I am doing this because it is who I am, and I won't be true to myself if I do anything else." I remember the moment I felt that being an entrepreneur was what I was meant to be. That is the moment when I simply knew I was who I was supposed to be. That is also the moment I gave up the excuses to justify NOT doing the things I was supposed to do. A powerful why, one that goes beyond money, will change the very nature of your neuropathways. It will open you up to operating in a flow state. This flow state narrows your focus, gets rid of the distractions, and builds your momentum toward success.

Chunk it down. The old strategy question is, "How do you eat an elephant?" The answer is and always has been, "One bite at a time." We are much better prepared to succeed when things are broken into bite-sized chunks. Instead of writing a book, write 1/5 of a chapter today. Instead of building an entire business, make 3 calls today. When you can break down your daily habits of success, you can manage what happens right now. It is thinking about all the things you need to get done that overwhelms you. Stop that shit. Instead, think about the couple of small things you need to get done in the next 3 hours. Stay focused on those things and success will chase you down. Make your success a series of bite-sized chunks. Then, keep biting off one chunk at a time.

Schedule it out. When I was starting out as a young executive, I felt overwhelmed with the number of things I was supposed to keep up with. I was in charge of multiple events, promotions, training programs, and was still expected to run my daily operations on top of those things. I learned the technique of "back-dating" in order to ensure I completed what I was supposed to when I was supposed to. This process is simply mapping out the amount of time required for a project and then determining how much time could be devoted to the project each day, week, or month. Next, I would determine how many weeks back from the end date I needed to start. Finally, I would place the chunked time on the calendar. This makes the process manageable as well as predictable.

Get some leverage. One of the things that has consistently helped me to find success is to let other people know when my deadline is for a book, or a project. I have even gone so far as to write out a check to an organization that makes me want to throw up in my mouth a little with the end date of the project on the check. I give the check to one of my friends who has no trouble being an asshole and let them know to send it if I don't finish on time. I also set up rewards for myself if I do finish both the chunked sections and the entire project. Giving myself emotional leverage is a great way to ensure I keep moving forward. After all, we are all emotional creatures at our core. I build up positive emotional leverage toward completing the tasks (rewards) and negative emotional leverage toward not completing the tasks (punishments). Since we do things for our own emotional reasons, pick some things that would be particularly motivating for you.

If you don't have time, scratch that... if you don't make time right now to do what is necessary, you won't have time later to do what you would like to do. Entrepreneurs and Intrapreneurs live like others won't so that later in life they can live like others can't. Sometimes it is necessary to take time out of our thinking. What I mean is that we must eliminate the time we get to think about whether or not we should do the thing or things we put on the calendar. I use "ready, set, go" from my childhood races with friends. When it is time to do something and I find myself hesitating, I simply say, "ready, set, go" and I move into the project. You need some kind of a motivator. You can count down to launch, repeat a mantra, or just ready, set, and go towards the finish line. Whatever you pick, pick something to take the thought time out of whether or not it makes sense to chase your dream and just chase the damn thing!

I like 'em cheap and easy

We unnecessarily complicate things in order to make things hard on ourselves. When writing your future, remember to make things as cheap on you and your resources as possible and accept that things can and should be easy. I had a conversation just this morning with a fellow entrepreneur. We were talking about a business idea that we both think will be fantastic. The thought I had was related to ways to minimize cost and effort in the launch of the new venture. So many people say things like "go big or go home" or let's make sure we are "all in." I have found in my couple of decades of running successful businesses that ego kills success. It kills success because people begin to feel invulnerable, unstoppable, and then they take uncalculated risks. I am all for risk. I am just even more for taking a risk that has the highest likelihood of success. Simplify your future and be able to explain it in such a way that anyone and everyone can understand it on the first try.

When you lay out the concept of your company or creative endeavor, you need to be able to explain it in such a way that the average 5th grader gets it. If you start with, "well, it is really hard to explain," then you are very likely going to fail. Easy is about whether or not your idea makes any sense. I help people find the potential inside of themselves and share it with the world. I have a contracting buddy who makes old houses new again. I have an artist friend who takes a blank canvas and reveals the beauty that was always meant to be there. If you know what you do and why you do it, make sure you can explain it in such a way that others go, "that makes perfect sense." Stay focused on the easy understanding of your concept and others will embrace your ideas.

Are those real?

The future plans we have are only real when we push ourselves to accept them as if they already are.

You are who you are because you defined yourself as who you are. You have made a series of choices that landed you in this exact place at this exact time. What is for you is what you saw for you. If you are in lack, you focused on the lack portion of life at a subconscious level. When you write your future, it must be present tense. It must be real to you. It must be who you already are. Once your vision of your success is real in your conscious awareness, your subconscious will take over and arrange the opportunities necessary for your success.

The process you should follow to make the future real right now is the T.E.V.A. model.

Thoughts begin in our conscious awareness. We choose what to think of ourselves. From that choice, we push suggestions into the subconscious mind. The subconscious seeks out ways to validate the new impression. By using auto-suggestion, or a repetition of your "I Am" statements first thing every morning, you are able to build the conscious and chosen belief of your success. Next is the emotional connection to the new image of self.

Emotions validate a belief. By holding on to the emotion of the new image, we are able to validate the belief at a subconscious level. Our thoughts and emotions/feelings must be in alignment with one another. If we think one way and feel another, we will tend to go with the feeling. Your future must be created in both thought and emotion in order to become real.

Vision is formed from our thoughts and emotions. When we buy into our own concept of the future, we see a vision of who we really are. If you are you 5 years in the future, are you still really you? That isn't a trick question. The reality is, you will always be you. You are the you of 5 years in the past as well as 5 years in the future. When you can create the image of that amazing version of yourself 5 years out, you are able to cling to the truth of you being you. Once the vision is solidified, the actions to attain that accepted vision become natural.

Actions are the bridge from the invisible to the visible. You have thought of your future, felt the glory of your future, and accepted a vision of you in that new state, now you must simply act. I often look at people who have attained a higher level of success than me and ask, "What have they done that I have not done?" That question helps me understand the resources required to become that level of success. If you know the formula for success another person has followed, then apply the formula in the same manner, you will receive predictable results. Build your bridge to your future through right daily action!

Record The Good Stuff

I would be remiss in a chapter on writing the future if I did not remind you of the importance of writing out your thoughts, affirmations, visions, and plans. When we take pen to paper, we activate another portion of our brain and engage all three learning styles within us. Journaling is the active process of managing our emotional states and resolving our issues. Doing this has the physiological benefit of strengthening our immunity. Journaling promotes the strengthening of t-lymphocytes which help in warding off disease and keeping us healthy.

I have found that writing through a problem and learning to process my day allows me to stay focused on my future. When I write about what I am thinking and feeling, I reaffirm my direction for the future. I process my struggles as if I am having a conversation with myself. My journal might resemble that of Oscar Wilde, who never left home without his journal, because I embody more than one persona as I write with myself. I talk through my challenges and answer myself with the better version of me. I argue back and forth with the little whiny shithead who sometimes tries to come out. I push myself toward my goal and pull myself out of stress. All of this is a beautifully written play between the character who is the better version of me and the villain who creates problems in my mind.

However you journal is up to you. You can have a conversation with yourself or simply write out your affirmations every day. Taking the time to organize your thoughts, feelings, visions, and action plans will make all the difference in the world. I do realize it takes a little time to journal. I usually spend 5 to 10 minutes journaling first thing in the morning. Every now and then, I need to pick the journal back up and work through an issue. I am the master of my fate and the captain of my soul because I repeatedly say so. When you accept the truth that you are who you are and where you are because you have chosen to be there, you take ownership for the things that move you forward. Writing out your future every day keeps you on track, builds the reality of your future vision, and creates a clear pathway to success. You are worth the effort!

9 G.D. Success – Goal Digger Success

Goal Digger Success

I know the gold-digger version of this statement is negative, whereas in my version, the goal digger is actually a good thing. I end up having the song by Kanye West, ft. Jamie Foxx, stuck in my head when I see this chapter title. It's a good beat, but it reminds me that someone who is just after the money to the exclusion of a mission is just a gold digger and not a goal digger. Being a goal digger is about learning how to dig deep inside of you in order to find the fuel necessary to keep going when things get tough. It is about building the fire inside of you and then directing that fire toward the actions that matter most.

When we begin to look at the goals that matter most, we have to seek balance in our pursuits. Too many goals and we crumble. Too few goals and we are uninspired. It is the right mix of goals that brings fulfillment. In a recent conversation with another entrepreneur, we discussed our financial successes and the reasons behind those successes. He and I have both worked hard to provide a lifestyle for our families that is a bit more comfortable. We have both focused on taking a good amount of time off and being present with our kids, our spouse, and our community. This focus on balanced success is what has made the journey worth it. When I first started in business, I had the wrong idea about what success meant for me. I thought I needed to demonstrate how many hours I could work and how hard I could hustle. I did well for the business, but I dumped so much money back into the business that I didn't do well for me. So, I did what I had seen other business people do, I just doubled down and worked harder and spent more money. One quick lesson for you is that when you find yourself in a hole that you have dug, digging faster and deeper never gets you out of the hole. Step one is to put down the damn shovel and get a better set of goals.

A few years into the journey, I put down the shovel and started evaluating the things that actually brought me a profit. I got rid of almost half of the things I was doing and saw my profits rise significantly. I was bringing in a large gross revenue and ending up with a small net revenue at the end of each year before this evaluation happened. The next year, I ended up with a large net revenue and a truckload of dirt to fill the hole I had dug earlier. I kept that focus and began to set goals for profitable activity instead of just for activity. I created rules like only allowing myself to be on two non-profit boards at a time. I also became very picky about where I spent my time so as to maximize that exposure and to benefit my goals in business. I learned how to create monthly revenue and to make systems that would create predictability. I set goals for vacations, for learning, for exercise, for meditation time, and more. I got so excited about the benefits of goal setting about 5 years into business that I sat goals for almost everything I was doing.

Too much of a good thing is still too much. I discovered there was a balance between goal setting and goal tracking. When I set too many goals to keep up with, I simply stopped keeping up. This led me to setting themed goals for myself in each of my domains of life. I would set a single word to guide my life for the year and a theme for each of my domains in life. I was able to keep up with themes and a word for each of the years after that. I found that once I discovered the right themes for my life, success began to find me more easily. I love to grow and develop and prosper and achieve at higher levels. I have, however, discovered that success is not just about money. Success in achieving your goals is about who you become along the journey. The money, the stuff, or whatever else you end up with are simply byproducts of great goal setting.

Whatever You Want

A friend of mine's dad used to tell him, "You can do whatever you want, but if you do, you may not be able to do whatever you want anymore." Keith Paschal was the dad telling his son Brad this advice. I love this! With our goals, there is always something we will need to give up. Ralph Waldo Emerson wrote about this in his essay, *The Law of Compensation.* In this essay, Emerson discusses the truth behind one's willingness to give up time, effort, relationship, or whatever the cost may be in order to acquire the thing that matters most to them. Early in the essay, Emerson eloquently states "… in changing moon and tidal wave, glows the feud of want and have." There is a battle inside of each of us raging for control. This battle is between wanting and having. Too often, people want something, but they want something else more. We even make fun of ourselves for this incessant battle between the wills with shirts like the one I saw in an airport recently which said, "Abs are great, but have you tried tacos?" It's funny, but it is also a sad truth. We know what it would take to achieve our dreams. We set the want goal to get there, but we often forget to accept the truth of the activity required to achieve the have side of the goal.

Not long after the previous phrase, Emerson states, "power to him who power exerts." We think of people who have wealth and success and often assume they were just blessed with it. I had one frustrated entrepreneur look at me and say, "You're an asshole man, because you don't understand how hard it is to be successful. Success is just easy for you. The rest of us have to work so damn hard at it." I did call bullshit on him because I did the work to find my success. What he really meant was that I did not understand how hard it was to work hard and then self-sabotage so that I could stay in struggle and be pissed off at those who chose to succeed. That also wasn't true though because I did my share of self-sabotage in the beginning. I just chose to put down the sabotage shovel and do what worked instead. The opening prose flows into Emerson's discourse on the subject of compensation and how he understood the trade of one thing for another. That is what goal setting is all about. It is about understanding what you are willing to give up in order to have the things you desire. When you consider your goals, what are you willing to let go of in order to have the end result of the goal?

I have been willing to give up a portion of money I could have earned in order to have time with my family. I have been willing to give up time with my family in order to earn the income I desired. I have been willing to give up time early in the morning and late at night in order to trade my knowledge for another's personal growth. I have banged away on a keyboard when I could have been zombified in front of a television soaking up entertainment. For anything you wish to achieve, anything worthwhile, will require you to give something in return. This is the law of compensation. Make no mistake, it is a law, not a suggestion.

Think about baseball

There are really four areas that one must be concerned with in setting goals for success. They are psychological, personal, physical, and professional. I put them in order of their impact on our lives. If you think about running the bases of a baseball diamond, they go from 1st, to 2nd, to 3rd, to Home in order to score any points. Our goals should go in order as well, but we are often trying to stay just on home plate, focusing on our professional goals.

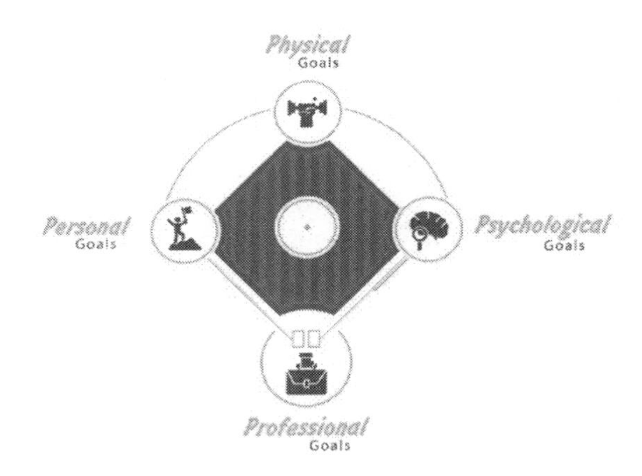

Regardless of the health of a man, if he has problems psychologically, he will not survive. Our psychological well-being is the most important aspect of who we are. It encompasses our spiritual connection, or mental stability, and the peace we experience in this life. The second most important aspect of your goal setting relates to your personal goals. Without achieving something of personal significance, the rest of your existence is for naught. After your personal goals come your physical goals. If you are rich and yet have no health, you will gladly trade your riches for a longer and healthier existence. Finally, your professional goals bring home the win by covering all the bases.

I do realize this order of goals is different from what most self-help gurus would tell you. Most of the authors and speakers out there are telling you how to find money so that you can have personal goals achieved, so that you can be healthy and psychologically well. It simply doesn't work that way, though. Your well-being begins with psychology, moves to physical, then to personal, and finally to professional. I think the wrong order of goal pursuits is the very reason so many people are hustling and yet unfulfilled in that hustle. I am going to take you through the process of understanding your goals in the TARGET section of this chapter and then help you map out how to write your goals in such a way that you can and will achieve them if you are willing to follow your own plan.

TARGET on my back

Think from the end to the beginning. This is the first step in achieving anything of significance. I find that most people set a goal because it sounds like the thing that will impress others or will "show them the money," but they don't think about what achieving the goal means. When you step back from the goal and begin to think about things from an end result perspective, you gain insight into why the goal is important. I have mentioned the importance of <u>WHY</u> several times in this book already. The why of your goal will tap into the limbic center of the brain instead of remaining just in the pre-frontal cortex. This means that your why stimulates emotions instead of just logic. You will need both in order to find success, but it all begins with that feeling. Take a moment and think about one of your goals. What would life be like for you if you achieved the goal? What would you feel like? How impressed and in awe of you would the people around you be? Get that image in your mind as if it has already happened. Now, think backwards from that achieved goal.

The process of thinking backwards should play much like a movie that we have hit a slow rewind on. When we are scrubbing backwards through a movie, we get to see every action taken in reverse. It helps to build the plot line from the end back to the beginning. As the movie is playing backward in your mind, take note of each of the steps you would have had to follow in order to achieve the success you have achieved in your vision. Take note of how long each step would have taken. Write down the amount of time for each step so that you can understand when you would need to start in order to finish on time. Once you have outlined what steps you would have to take and how much time each of the steps would have taken, you will have a timeframe for the work required. All you have to do after that is determine how much time you can and will devote each month or week or day toward the accomplishment of your goal. This roadmap is what most people, top executives included, never put together. They set a goal, paint a beautiful word picture of it, and then never do shit to plan for the attainment of the goal. You have to map out the time required and schedule it! You have to! I am drilling this in because you will allow the world to take over your time if you don't make it a "have" to and not a "want to."

Assess your skills and skill gaps. As you step back from your movie of success, you will evaluate the things required for you to achieve that end goal. If you are raising money for a new venture, you need to become adept at the art and skill of presenting your idea. If you are planning on becoming a corporate trainer, you need to have a plan for the number of books on your chosen subject you will read in order to become proficient. Your skills are the list of things you have to offer the world that directly relate to your business. Your skill gaps are the things that you know you need to be able to offer, but don't yet have the skills mastered in that area. For example, when I was 19 years old and in college, I decided to start doing direct sales through a multi-level marketing company. I had never done this before, but I had seen my aunt sell things through Amway when I was a kid. I never saw her have a party or draw circles, just sell stuff. I really liked the guy who was recruiting me, and I trusted him. He has since passed, but his name was Dub Pritchett, and I learned a great deal from him. I sat down and made a list of what skills I had and what skill gaps I had. It looked something like this…

My Skills	My Skill Gaps
Good at sales	I don't know a lot of people in this new town
Connect quickly with others	I have only sold in an environment where people come to me
I have a reason for succeeding	I don't have a lot of extra money
I am a great speaker	I am taking a full load in college
I have a product I believe in	
I have a plan with daily actions to take	
I am incredibly persistent, even when people tell me no	
I am mostly comfortable with rejection	
I don't know a lot of people here so who gives a shit if they don't like me	

In the end, there was more on the skill side than on the gap side, so I went for it. I made a decent living at it for a couple of years as I was finishing up college. It was a good bit more income than I would have made working at a minimum wage job and quite a few less hours than I would have put in. As I got started, I had to stay focused on the things I claimed as my skills and I had to stay focused on overcoming the gaps in skills I had identified. By doing this, I kept my mind focused on the things that mattered most. We have to be careful because our minds will often wander back to the gaps and forget that we ever even talked about having skills. Far too many entrepreneurs, MLM-ers, writers, and other creative types will quit because they have forgotten what made their choice the right one in the first place. That demon of self-doubt creeps in and kicks your ass if you don't keep him at bay. Do your part to set yourself up for success by mapping out the things you are good at and have skill in doing.

Recruit the resources and talent you need. There will be things you might not know. There will be things you are not that skilled in doing. That's okay. If you are a jack of all trades, you are likely a master of none of them. Your job is to find your niche and then find talent to fill in the other areas required. I am a writer, trainer, speaker, and coach. I am not a great CPA. That is the reason I hired someone who was gifted in that area and still use a fantastic CPA as well. If I spent a lot of time on my accounting, I would not be spending enough time with the things that I am best at. When we recruit talent, we do so to fill a specific need, not to simply add employees. Your ego can get in the way if you let it. I know because mine has several times over the years. I would hire someone because I would be able to look at the company and be impressed with the growth in people and expanded services. Quite often, I would be very disappointed in the person I hired because I hired a cheap person instead of the right person. There are multiple ways to get the talent resources you need other than just hiring people. I am not opposed to hiring, but I want to make sure there isn't any other way to get the job done with great talent and no more money first.

I have used several outsourcing sites over the years. Two of my favorites are upwork.com and fiverr.com right now. Upwork used to be known as Odesk, but it is designed as a way to recruit talent to help you without any geographic restrictions and without having to hire the person as an employee. I would encourage you to be careful when you do this because it will either be a great experience, or you will want to get on a plane and track down the little shit who said they could do the job and then didn't deliver. I always recommend that you do a small project with a contractor before you jump all in. It is critically important that you actively manage anyone that is doing work for you. If you don't, you will get hosed in the end. This is true of employees, contractors, seasonal employees, or anyone you hire to accomplish work for you. If you aren't sure how to manage and lead, go to Amazon and get a copy of my book Yay! I'm A Supervisor! Each of us will need help from time to time in order to accomplish our goals. If we are not willing to find the resources and talent necessary, we will produce a half-ass job that leaves us and the client disappointed. Your goals and dreams are worth the calculated investment. Do NOT go spend all your money on other people thinking they will do the whole thing for you. You will very likely just be giving away all of your money if you do. Instead, use your talents and skills to the fullest, and THEN go recruit the help you need. You go first, though.

Give it emotions mixed with a little logic. With our goals and dreams, we must have the right emotional push behind them in order to make it through the tough times. Our objective is to align our cognitive processes with our emotive processes. It is the blend of thought and feeling that pushes us in the right direction and repels us from the wrong direction.

ERW – Emotional reasons why will work on both a positive and a negative spectrum. On the positive side of things, we map out how we would feel if everything we wanted worked just like it was supposed to work. This means we need to list out what we have accomplished and then attach an emotional state to each of the accomplishments, and then describe why we would feel the way we indicated with each accomplishment. Really lean into this and soak up the feeling side of things as you map out your future. Once you have gone through the positive side of things, it is time to step into the dark side. With each accomplishment, map out how you would feel if you did not accomplish what you wanted to accomplish. Think primarily about how you would feel if you chose not to put in the effort necessary. Don't focus on whether or not you can accomplish it. Instead, assume it is completely possible and then look at how you would feel if you intentionally did not go for it. After you identify the feeling, describe why you would feel as bad as you would feel for not going for the dream or the goal. The emotion is where most of your power exists for getting leverage over yourself. Without the emotion, the logic will do very little to move you forward.

LRW – Logical reasons why are how we explain to ourselves and others our decision to keep moving forward. When I left my job that paid well in order to be an entrepreneur with no safety net, I needed to be able to explain to well-meaning friends and family who questioned my sanity. You will do the same thing with logic that you did with emotion. You must be able to explain the justification behind the goal. This means outlining the positive impact that will happen when each of your goals is achieved. After you explain the positive impact, you need to map out why this impact is important in your life. On the dark side of logic, you need to explain what happens to you when you intentionally give up the pursuit of a goal or dream. How does that impact you, your family, your friends, your mental state? Finally, why would you be impacted the way you would if you chose not to pursue each of the goals? When you put all of this on paper, it gives you leverage over yourself and helps you keep your thinking on track.

Eyes wide open is a statement of focus related to the measurement of your goals. So often, our goals are so non-descript that they are almost impossible to measure. A great goal statement makes measurement possible. An open mind makes measurement likely. You will need to have the roadmap in front of you from the first step, "think from the end to the beginning." You should have a timeline and a way to measure the success of each step. When you let go of your ego and allow yourself to truly measure your progress, you begin to realize that there are certain things you must do every single day in order to be successful. Vilfredo Pareto came up with what he called the "Pareto Principle." Most of us know this principle as the 80/20 rule. This rule demonstrates that 20% of the things you do will produce 80% of the results you achieve. When we measure, a big part of what we are looking for is whether or not we are staying focused on the 20% of things that produce the most results or whether we are getting sucked into the vortex of the 80% that keeps us very busy… and broke. Measure yourself daily, weekly, monthly, quarterly, and annually. When you stay fully focused on doing the things that produce for you and your business, you get rid of a ton of things that are just time dumps. I do realize that many of those time dumps are the things that are fun to do, but they don't produce success. Be careful how many of them you allow into your productive time!

Talk about your goal/baby and do it on a regular basis. Your goal is uniquely yours. You need to let people know what you are doing and how excited you are about accomplishing it so that they will give you shit if you don't. You need as much pressure as possible, particularly for things that are not required by someone else. When I had not been a runner in over a decade and decided I wanted to run a 5K, I started telling people that I was going to run a 5K. When they started asking me when I was going to do this, I was forced to choose a date and a race. Once I chose the date and the race, I mapped out what it would take to go from not a runner to being a runner. I have friends whom I knew would call me and ask how it was going. I also knew that those same friends would give me grief if I did not finish the race. As a result, I built even more pressure for myself to ensure the race was finished when I said it would be. This is the same reason I tell people when my next book is coming out. I need the pressure of others to ensure I hit my targets. I own my own business. If I don't hit a target, my paycheck is impacted, but I can't get fired by any of my friends. I love positive impacts on my check, and I loathe negative ones. I will use whatever tools are at my disposal to ensure the good happens and the bad does not. What about you? Are you willing to talk about your goal? Are you willing to apply a little extra pressure? I hope so, and we'll see!

The Perfect Line Works Every Time

The manner in which you write your goals matters greatly. There are three components that must be present in the perfect goal statement. What will you get? What will you give in order to get it? Why are you going after it? Two of these three questions are often ignored completely.

Most people will talk about what they will get. They will even add in how awesome it will be when they get it, but they almost never talk about the other two components, and they are critical to your success. I am so not screwing around on this one. You HAVE to outline what you are going to give in order to get what you want to get. If you don't outline the trade off, you are setting yourself up for failure. When a person wants to start a business, they dream of the success but often don't even think about the effort required. I ask "wantrapreneurs" what they would be willing to give up in order to attain their dream of entrepreneurial success. Most of the people I have talked to over the years want the freedom but are unwilling to sacrifice. We have already talked about you being able to have whatever you want but know that you are giving up something else if you do. Everything in this life is a trade-off. I can tell you from personal experience, you need to be aware up front of the effort you are willing to give. I could be much more successful than I am currently if, and only if, I was willing to give more than I am giving. What will you give?

The third question relates to why you are going after the goal you are going after. I have found that when I cannot explain the why, I never reach the goal. I have set goals in the past that were fantastic, sounded great, and were doable. I have had to come face to face with why I was going for the goal in the first place. When I explained my reason as being related to pleasing others, or doing something because it would impress someone else, I lacked the steam to produce. However, when I was able to see my own reason for going for a goal, I was driven at the right level to succeed. Why are you doing this? That question will either build a fire in your belly, or it will be a lukewarm cup of water in your belly. I get rid of any lukewarm dreams and keep the ones that have me burning with a desire to succeed!

Put Grinding In The Back Seat

We obsess too much about the goals having to be hard. Although I do work diligently, I ensure that I am aiming for the right goals and not grinding for the sake of grinding. I see so many people talking about how they hustle all day, every day, and never back down. I also see many of those same people busily going broke. We have to step back from the goal and ask ourselves if we are focusing on the thing that matters the most. When I first went into business, I figured people would respect me more if I was incredibly busy. So, I was always incredibly busy. I hustled in my marketing, my sales, and my volunteer work. I was grinding away 24/7/365. I didn't take days off. I worked like others wouldn't so that I could live like others couldn't. Hell, I barely survived that shit, but that's how I lived. I remember making a new decision about 4 years into business. I had increased my revenues every year and somehow found ways to lose a little more money and go a little further into debt each year as well. That one decision changed everything for me. I finally decided to find balance. I decided that having a goal of taking more vacation was just as valid as a goal of making more money. When I learned to stay balanced, I began to reduce the time spent on things that did not produce revenue. I also got rid of things that did not produce a high enough margin. In doing this, I made money for the first time while also taking several weeks of vacation.

I remember reading about Tim Ferris and his rat race of a pace he was keeping before writing The

Four Hour Workweek. He started going through the worst-case scenario planning and looked at what it would take to actually go on vacation. This was after my decision, by the way. In his story, he said that he was in a panic thinking about how his business would fail if he took time off. As he looked at how he would handle any of the situations that might go wrong, he found a clear path to taking 30 days off to travel abroad. This 30-day trip turned into an 18-month world tour that also resulted in a best-selling book.

It is important to stay fully focused on finding success. The mistake we make is in just staying fully busy. As I am writing this, I am one day away from going to Vegas for a guy weekend with one of my very best friends. We started doing these around 2012 and plan to do a trip or two a year from now on. I have to recover from the grind. I have to find my success in everything I do. I can't just find it in grinding at work to achieve my financial goals. Success is defined differently from one person to another. For some, it is defined as having more money or toys. For others, it is defined as having the lifestyle that affords fun along with the work. When I started setting fun goals along with money goals, I found out that money was chasing me down. It wanted to be a part of my life. I believe my subconscious mind refused to just gather money unless it got to express it in a manner that was fitting. I do think we are supposed to grind away at our goals. I don't, however, think that grinding is the goal. The goal is becoming the person we were always meant to be.

I was always supposed to be a writer, trainer, speaker, and business coach. I was always supposed to be a husband, father, grandfather, and son. I was always supposed to be a friend and a support. What were you always supposed to be? The grinding that you do to achieve your goals should be secondary, not primary. When you keep it in the back seat, you are keeping the best version of you in the driver's seat. This enables you to work for a real reason, not just for the sake of working your ass off. Digging in on your goals doesn't mean giving up the thing that means the most. It means balancing out your goals so that you have the greatest shot at happiness and success.

This balance provides a mechanism for your success. It also helps you to remember that goals are not attained in Hail Mary plays the majority of the time. Goals should be on a map with a specific target of things to do each day and should be predictable. By keeping things in front of you on a daily basis, you are keeping the wrong things out of your way. Our ego often gets in our way, leading us to try to put someone else in their place by showing how much of a bad ass we are for putting in crazy hours. Get that shit in check… NOW! Your success can be mapped into a daily plan of action that leads to weekly success, which leads to monthly, quarterly, annual, and lifelong success. What are the things that matter most each and every day? Do those first! Then, and only then, you can move on to the other miscellaneous stuff on your to-do list.

Where The Magic Happens

You have to create a personal mantra and a new belief system to get your business strategy moving in the right direction. The magic happens when you learn to use auto-suggestion on a regular basis to condition the thoughts you are pushing into your subconscious mind. I put together a planner that asks you to write "I AM" statements each day. It outlines what needs to be done for the day in the way of tasks and schedule. Then, it provides for a place to take notes and plan out the next day. You can find the planner by searching for "#GSD Planner" on Amazon. The magic happens when you remember who you are at your best. You only become that which you are already aware of being. Some of my favorite I AM statements are as follows…

I am balanced.

I am sought after.

I am a positive influence on all that I meet.

I am focused on what matters.

I am successful.

I am at peace.

I am a great husband.

I am a great father.

I am an incredible grandfather.

I am in control of myself and my destiny.

I am a kick-ass trainer!

You can pick whatever I AM statements you want, but you need to begin filling your mind with the right kinds of statements and influences. What you put into your mind will determine what you achieve in this life. Be very careful how you program yourself. After all, you are the master coder of your fate. If you allow garbage into your code, your chances of success, your operating system for life, will likely crash. If you fill your subconscious operating system with good, clean, well-written, positive, success-focused code, your operating system will be solid, and your success will be automatic. Auto-suggestion is simply using these positive affirmations every single day to push the right image of self from the conscious mind into the subconscious mind. Doing this builds your success code and gets rid of the garbage. You've got this! Program away!

10 Stop Giving 110%

Come on Holland!

I heard multiple coaches yell, "Come on Holland, Give 110%", when I was young and in sports. I do realize that I often viewed the world differently than most of my friends and acquaintances growing up, but my thought response to this admonition was a little odd even to me. I used to think, "If I do that, I am taking away someone else's opportunity." When we operate outside of what is our best, even if that means trying to do more than our minds or bodies would allow, we set ourselves up for failure. We set ourselves up to burn out and we often take others down with us. My belief is that each of us should perform according to our capabilities and our bandwidth. This also means that we should not give only 70%. Finding your balance of what your personal best is can take a little time. Once you discover your best, however, you will never be able to go back to the way things used to be. I will never work all day every day without a break again. I will never settle for good enough again. I will give my best and not give a shit about what someone else's best is. I will go with the proverbial flow that I was created for. How about you?

The motion of the ocean

Each of us has a rhythm that is ideal for our success. By managing the rhythm and learning to work with our Circadian Rhythm as well as our working rhythm, we position ourselves for success. Your Circadian Rhythm is the 24-hour cycle that your brain and body operate within. You cycle through this rhythm every day. Some people are set for early morning. Some are set for late nights. Some are set for 6 hours of sleep per night. Some are set for 9 hours. One is not right and the other wrong. They are each unique to the person who expresses the rhythm. I think we often get caught up in trying to get others to be just like us or trying to be just like someone else. When we learn to be okay with being ourselves, we discover the model of work best for us.

First thing in the morning, we are naturally better at cramming to develop short-term memories. In the afternoon, we are naturally more coordinated because our bodies are at a peak temperature and we are least likely to injure ourselves. We perform manual tasks best in the afternoon as well. Mid-morning, we do best in transferring things to long-term memory. These are standards that science has taught us. Studies of thousands of people have outlined "best practices" for when we should do things. Science has also outlined things that are contradictory to these statements. One thing I know to be true for me is that I don't fit the definition of normal. I think that normal is simply a setting on my dryer and doesn't define much else in my life. I wrote my first two books during the hours of 11 PM and 4 AM because that is when I had time, and I am fairly creative at night. My dad used to tell me that nothing good happens after midnight. I think he just knew that people got overly creative with their ideas after midnight and would often jack some shit up in a quest for creative expression. You have to find your flow.

Psychologist, Mihaly Csikszentmihalyi (pronounced Me-hi Chick-sent-me-hi), talks about how the mind achieves a flow-state, or what athletes call being "in the zone." In his book Flow, he indicates the change in the processing of the conscious mind (Csikszentmihalyi, 2008). The conscious mind narrows its focus down from full capacity to as little as 25% input. When the conscious mind blocks more of the outside inputs and stays centered on more of the critical inputs, we lose track of the rest of the world around us and, consequently, achieve a flow state. Many writers achieve a flow state when they are in the middle of their creative expression. Many painters achieve this flow state when they are transferring their image onto a canvas from their minds. It is, from my experience, the most freeing state to exist within and one that I pursue as often as possible.

The ocean has a flow state. It is powerful and beautiful and creative and in its purest expression of self. It does not worry about what others are thinking of it. It does not change to please others. It does not try to offend others to prove a point. It does not know that others exist. It simply "is." Your perfect state of being is in expressing yourself as yourself. When we try to express ourselves in the standard of another person or in the manner that someone else has indicated is "the only acceptable way," we are miserable. I want to be fully me.

I have used a story in my talks on finding the right fit in life that describes forest animals and their journey to become more intelligent. The best I can tell, this story evolved from a quote from Albert Einstein. "Everybody is a genius. But, if you judge a fish by its ability to climb a tree, it will live its whole life believing that it is stupid." I am both genius and simpleton, depending only on the manner in which I am being judged.

The Story

There once was a young group of forest animals discussing ways to be more successful in their endeavors. A squirrel, a fish, a bird, and a rabbit decided they would approach a wise old owl and ask the owl if he would be willing to be the headmaster of a school for them. The owl, knowing he had much to offer since he had been observing the world from a broader perspective, agreed to teach the young animals. They all agreed on a start date of the following Monday. First thing Monday morning, the owl decided he would take the animals through each of the general skills required for their success. Since there was a river running through the middle of the forest, he chose to begin the lessons with swimming. The fish seemed so natural in this environment. It was almost as if he was the only genius in the class. He swam upstream, downstream, across the stream, and could maneuver incredibly well in the water. The squirrel paddled like crazy and made it across the river, while the bird flittered across the surface of the water and survived for the next lesson. The rabbit was the final animal to go through the first day's lesson. He jumped in the water and went right to the bottom. He pushed with his powerful back legs and sprung out of the water, only to sink back to the bottom. He would sink and spring, sink and spring, and finally made it out of the water on the other side. He did require some help from both the fish and the bird to survive, though. As the students lined up to get their grades for the day, the fish got an A+. The squirrel got an A-. The bird got a C+, and the rabbit received a failing grade. The owl pulled the rabbit aside and expressed his disappointment in his abilities as a forest animal. He told him he would need to practice swimming every day until he became good at it. On Tuesday, he tried and failed. On Wednesday, he tried and failed. On Thursday, he got more of the same frustration. By the time he finished week one, he went to the headmaster and let him know he was simply not smart enough for school. The headmaster agreed and welcomed his resignation from school to live the rest of his life in struggle.

I feel bad for the rabbit every time I tell this story. I also have to wonder, though. What would have happened if the headmaster would have started with hopping instead of swimming? Would the rabbit have been a huge success? I think the rabbit would have believed he was a genius and the fish would have "flopped." We spend so much of our time trying to be a fish, when we are a rabbit, or squirrel when we are a bird. The objective isn't to become something or someone you are not. The objective is to find your flow and your fit in this world and then live into your greatness.

Each of us has greatness inside of us. Each of us has something we are creative geniuses at. You are a giant unless you label yourself as a grasshopper in the presence of giants. I am a gifted writer, speaker, and business coach. I was good at writing stories and speaking as a kid, and I loved to do those things. What were the things you did well as a kid? What were the things you loved to do? Who is the creative child at your core? That is where you find your flow. I admittedly look at other people who are in their element and think, I should do what they do… at times. It isn't what they do that I, or anyone else really wants. It is the flow state. To be in flow, you must act on the things where your natural genius exists. You must ACT!

A – Advance your skills in the thing you love to do. When you take the time to become better at the thing you love, you find passion in the work. We were made to work. We were made to become better and better at the things we find important.

C – Creation is the natural state of mankind. We were created to create a full version of ourselves. When we create, we bring life into the world. The act of bringing life, or birthing ideas produces a natural state of gratefulness as well as positive pride. Every day, we must create something that represents who we are.

T – Think! Think! Think! We are thinking creatures. That is the key distinction between us and the animal kingdom. We have the capacity for thinking and planning and rationalizing thought. We are not ruled by our amygdala or by the limbic center of the brain. We developed a pre-frontal cortex, a new brain, which allows us to think long-term and to take deliberate actions in the face of contradictory information.

What keeps us from acting is becoming caught up in the fear of what others might think of us. We worry about looking like an idiot. We worry about being seen as someone who did not do what their parents wanted them to do. It is when we break free of the drama that we are able to find our rhythm. Earlier, I asked you to master the art of not giving a shit what others think of you. Truly giving up the need for approval is the final piece required to achieve a flow state in our lives. Stop giving 110% and stop giving a shit what others think. Start giving a shit about who you are and who you know you will be. Start being you, fully you, and only you!

Heroes – Victims – Villains

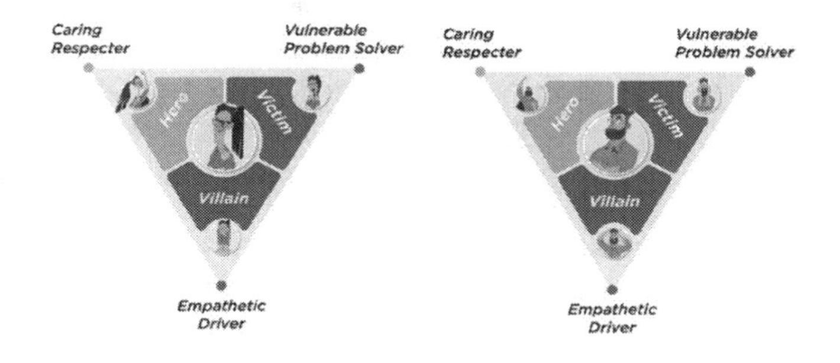

The drama triangle can kick anyone's ass. You need to be prepared for the challenge of getting and staying out of the vortex. This triangle gets the best of people every single day. You can pull up social media, particularly Facebook, right now and see victim after victim. A victim is someone who believes the world is out to get them, that their life sucks, and that others need to hear about it. They go out of their way to describe how much they cry, how much they are oppressed, or how the world simply cannot and does not understand them. Victims will seek out either a hero or a villain in order to validate the plight that is their life. Here is how a victim works. A triggering event happens in the person's life. The person labels the event as being some kind of an unfair attack or unfair circumstance in their life. They seek out a person or group to save them while simultaneously seeking out a person or a group to blame. Victims need both heroes and villains. They are the only one of the three areas of the drama triangle requiring both sides in order to exist. Most people who are stuck in victimhood are likely unaware of what they are doing. I am giving people the benefit of the doubt because we get conditioned at a very early age to either be fully in charge of ourselves, regardless of our circumstances, or we learn to play on the emotions of others to get our attention. Think about someone you know who seems to constantly need validation from others to get up and do life one more time. It shouldn't be too hard to come up with a few examples of this because it seems to be the rule more than the exception.

With the image of the person in your mind, think about the number of times you have seen or heard them talking about their plight in life. Think about the number of times you have had to build them up, encourage them, or simply let them know life was going to be okay. These are the sympathy victims who are in your mind now. The other type of victim is the one who is being held down by life, by others, by the system, or by some other ubiquitous force that is insurmountable. They need to be offended and hurt by the things happening in their life. Get a picture of this person in your mind and think about the number of times they talk or post about what someone is doing or trying to do to take advantage of them. There is more than one model of victimhood. Regardless of how a person is a victim, they see themselves being unable to overcome the circumstances of their life.

"Man is not the creature of circumstances, circumstances are the creatures of men. We are free agents, and man is more powerful than matter."

--Benjamin Disraeli

The only way a person gets themselves out of victimhood is to embrace the truth that circumstances do not control them. They must become vulnerable in their desire to solve problems and willing to accept full responsibility for who and where they are. My truth is that people are who they are and where they are because they have made a series of decisions that landed them in that exact spot in that exact moment. The vulnerable problem-solver accepts full responsibility for the problem and the part they have played in creating it. They stop seeking an external explanation and accept an internal explanation. This is not easy! This is a complete shift in perspective for the person and will likely come with sacrificing the version of themselves at the altar of success in order to grow out of this shithole of a wrong concept of self. Say it with me, "I am responsible for me. I am who I am and where I am because I made each decision along the way that landed me here. I am also capable of making a new decision right now that will change my world. My first act as a success is to believe I am fully responsible for myself and my success! I am in charge of me!" See, doesn't that feel better once the pain stops. It also reduces the amount of effort required for success when you accept your control over your own life. This leads to you positioning yourself to do the things that matter the most and avoid the things limiting you. You are fully capable of success as long as you are not a victim.

The second piece of the drama triangle is the hero. This is the role I find lots of people in and have found myself drawn to play as well. I like being the one to save the day. It feeds my ego and makes me think I am awesome. It is also just as much bullshit as being a victim. I create victims by trying to be a hero. I often even make myself into a victim by trying to play the hero to others. Here is basically how it works in hiring others.

A person comes to me and tells me they are in **need** of a job. They have had a string of bad luck that has left them in a bad place. They never tell me they have made a string of bad choices, just that they have had bad luck. I think about how great I am as a manager and leader and how great my cause is, then look at the poor wretched soul in need of my saving, then offer them a **chance**. This chance is me believing they are not capable and me not respecting the truth of them making their own choices. It is me buying into their bullshit victimhood story and helping them continue down the same awful path. I perpetuated them being a victim! Next, they go to work reluctantly because they really didn't want my job. They don't really want any job. They want to be able to continue being a victim, which means I will now be the hero for a minute, then I will be the new villain to them. When they start taking advantage of me, and they definitely will, I start feeling like a victim. I hate this because I am supposed to only be the hero. It never works to stay as just the hero because victims play both sides of the fence. When they start taking advantage of me by not doing their job, not going out and selling, not making good on their promises, they attempt to take advantage of my poor decision-making as a hero. I move as fast as possible out of being a victim, because I can't identify with that corner of the triangle, and I become a full-on, proud as hell of being it, in your face villain. I fire their sorry ass for not doing what I told them I wanted them to do.

If I don't care enough about others to only put them in a position of success, I am playing the hero. I need to be a caring respecter in order to make their success possible. I tell people to make good choices and demonstrate their potential before I hire them. I don't hire people who have demonstrated their victimhood. I do realize this narrows the field, but do you really want a wrong person in your organization, your down-line, or any other aspect of your life? I don't. They are exhausting! Respect people enough to hold them to a higher standard. They will either live into your standard or find another person who will allow them to be a victim. Drop the hero mask and pick up the caring respecter mask. This keeps your life on track and keeps you out of that corner of the drama triangle.

The final corner of the drama triangle is the villain. I immediately have images of the joker from batman when I think of a villain. This is the person who goes out of their way to make life worse for the people around them. Villains don't just see the cloud in every silver lining, they point out which cloud is yours and attempt to make you feel bad about it. They are masters at finding your flaws and exploiting those flaws. I know bosses who are villains and destroy the weekends of great employees everywhere. I know spouses who are villains and keep their insignificant other on the ropes at all times, leading to a miserable and beaten down existence for the victim in the scenario.

Villains need a victim to go after. They don't generally go after heroes because heroes are too busy finding a victim who will praise them for their greatness. They find people to take advantage of, to keep down, to exploit. There are lots of villains in the world, but they don't compare to the number of victims. After all, both villains and heroes need to find a victim to tend to. The pathway out of being a villain, if you are that kind of person or you find that the victim in your life requires that of you, is to be an empathetic driver. Empathy is the ability to view the world from the perspective of another person. It isn't about feeling sorry for them, that's sympathy. Sympathy keeps a victim a victim. Empathy provides understanding. Being a driver is about pushing a person to live into their potential even if they are fighting against success. I see more people who will fight to stay in victimhood than I do people who are fighting to get out of it. This is why being both empathetic and a driver are required to get out of villainhood. Some might call this tough love. I would agree with those folks. Who is it in your life that needs you to stop being forceful and telling them what to do? Who can you drive towards their decision for greatness? You are combining the three non-drama responses together in order to release the potential of others as well as your own. I have conversations in my journal regularly, pushing myself to be the person I was always intended to be. You may have to have some tough conversations with yourself as well. Respect your ability to succeed and your capability to make that choice. Be vulnerable and ask for help solving problems when you need help beyond your own abilities. See the world from multiple angles in your life, then be driven in taking action toward your own success. You should talk to yourself in the same manner you would talk to others. Be consistent about believing in each and every person's ability to choose their own path. Then, choose your path!

Emotions Suck… The Life Out of Business When They Are Uncontrolled

We burn up way too much energy trying to feel the right way before we take any action. When our emotions are out of control, they truly suck the life out of our business! When was the last time you woke up and felt like exercising, eating right, and taking time to meditate? If you are like most people, you only feel like doing those things after you have been doing them for a while. You experience the action before you experience the emotional activation. The word motivate originates from the German word, motivieren. It means to stimulate toward action. It does not say it has anything to do with feeling like taking action. We each need a way to get our negative emotions out of the way so that we take consistent action toward our goals. I don't feel like calling people to see if I can meet with them in order to get them as a client. I don't feel like reaching out to friends and family to tell them about the cool product I am on that is changing my life. These are the things that are keeping you in your broke-ass life and keeping you from being who you know you are at your core.

Get rid of the need for feeling by creating a daily game plan for your success. If I know I have to make 10 calls each and every day to get a speaking gig, it can become a part of my stimulated and required action. I schedule it out so as not to spend too much time thinking about it. When I first went into business, I needed a plan that would allow me to be automated for my own success. The way to do this for me was to know what I was going to do from 7:30 AM to 8:30 AM, from 9-10, and so on. Making 10 phone calls per day in order to get presentations set up typically took me under 1 hour when I followed my schedule. When I didn't follow my schedule, it would take me an hour to drink coffee and feel a little better about the idea. It would take me an hour after that to psych myself up and plan out my calls. After that, I would spend an hour prepping and researching each of the people I was going to call. Then, it was really close to lunch and I didn't want to screw up people's lunches, so I would wait till after lunch. After that, I would work my ass off to come up with more excuses why I couldn't call. I worked harder to fail than I would have to succeed. This is what it means to reduce your effort down to the effort that matters the most.

20% of what you do will get you 80% of the results you will achieve. My philosophy is and has been for some time now to do the 20% that matters before I do anything else. When you do this, you will find the majority of the things you were doing to be suddenly irrelevant. I have more success in less time by doing what matters and skipping what does not matter. Here is your simple litmus test for what to do.

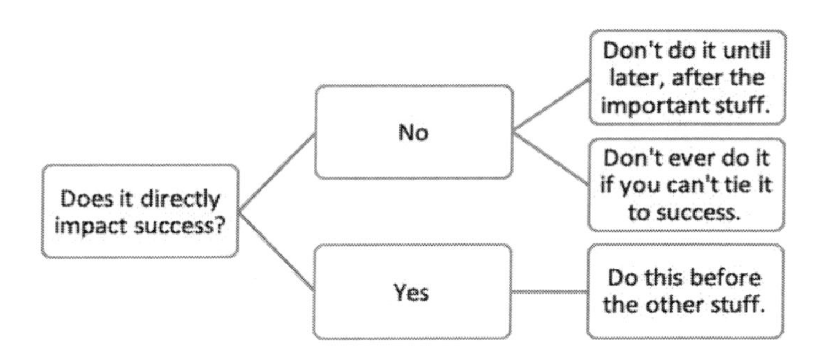

Lots of people need a decision matrix in order to keep themselves on track. I know I have had to step back from lots of the things I enjoyed doing and ask whether or not it was having a positive impact. This includes some of the "great opportunities for exposure" that people present to you. As a professional speaker, people approach me with lots of exposure opportunities. Here is the typical translation of that offer… "We aren't going to pay you and most of our people are too damn cheap to ever pay you, so will you give us your talent for free so that we can exploit it for our gain because we are villains." I like some of the people who ask this question of me, but I have found that it doesn't give me an opportunity very often. I have also found rules to be very helpful in limiting these time-sucks. I have a give-away budget which includes my time. Once the budget is reached, I don't give anything else away no matter what. I have also found that asking if I can promote myself on stage really lets me know whether or not they give a shit about my success. If the answer is no, they couldn't care less if I succeed. They just want free stuff. If the answer is yes, it might help me get to the place of success I am headed toward. I love speaking on stage for large MLM groups. Multi-level marketing people are hungry for growth and success. They are NOT kidding around because they are seeking a better life. This better life is won through the elimination of what doesn't work. Narrow your focus and up your game! You've got this!

Build In Protection

You have to build a protective barrier for your time and your efforts so that others don't destroy your ability to succeed. Don't take your neighbor to the doctor when you should be selling. Don't take time off during the day to run errands when you should be focused on success. Don't leave the internet turned on when you are trying to write. Those are some of the little barriers to help you achieve success. I do paperwork after 4 PM. I make calls during working hours. I train every day when possible. I write every day when possible. I build buffers into my time to keep people from taking advantage of me and my skills. If you are gifted at something, don't do it for free. Make sure you are able to monetize your time for success.

A few of the things I recommend are…

1. Be the boss of your technology. Turn off internet access when you should be focused on things not requiring internet.
2. Make your calls at the same time every day and make a consistent number each day. Being consistent about this keeps you from making excuses. As a side note, attempting to call and just getting a voicemail is not the same as making calls until you get ahold of 10 people, or whatever number you choose.
3. Reward yourself for doing what you are supposed to do. Knowing you get a reward, whether that is time to yourself, a quick YouTube break, or something that inspires you, will keep you focused on getting done what you need to get done.
4. Life is best before noon. Try to get all of the 20% done before noon anytime possible. Schedule the things that matter the most before you make it to lunch. I know the day gets away from some people, but it rarely does when you have a non-negotiable plan. All the important stuff should come first, not last.

Stop Knowing All The Answers

Collapse time by finding people who have already gone through the shit that you need to figure out and learn from them. Intelligence is your ability to learn from your own mistakes. When we go through any business challenge, we have the opportunity to evaluate the steps we followed as well as the lessons learned. As a leader, you should be continuously in learning mode. At the end of each challenge as well as the end of each defeat, I ask myself what I learned from the process. This attitude of learning allows me to reshape the meaning of a challenge. More importantly, it enables me to make sure I don't repeat the same mistake again. By learning the lessons failure can teach us, we are best prepared to get things done quicker, more efficiently, and right on the next try. If you want to really go to the next level, you collapse time further by learning from people who have already been there, done that, and gotten the proverbial t-shirt. There are thousands of books on just about any subject you could want to master. Read the books of people who have been around the block a time or two and apply their advice in your life. They have already made a bunch of mistakes. When you leverage the learning of multiple people, you go from being intelligent to being wise. Wisdom is simply your ability to learn from the mistakes of others so you don't have to make them yourself.

Hire a coach! They take the 10, 15, 20 or more years of work and collapse it into condensed learning. Much of what I do as a leader is based on what I have learned from my experiences as well as from the experiences of hundreds of other greats. I read every day. I learn from the masters, and I distill their lessons as well as my own into actionable plans for success. When we think we have to do everything ourselves, we miss out on the incredible experience offered by others. Stop giving more than you can give to achieve your success and start leveraging wisdom in achieving your greatness. As I write this, I have been in business for over 19 years. I have found life to get easier each year that I assimilate both intelligence and wisdom into my daily habits. I work fewer hours in a year now than I did in 6 months when I first went into business. I also do 3 times the revenue. That is not a brag. That is the power of learning. Next, I will explain a few of the lessons learned about how to get rid of the bandits stealing your most precious commodity… time.

Eliminate Time Bandits

We get so caught up in doing things that don't matter that we often forget to do the things that matter the most. Whether this is volunteering for a good cause, organizing our office in order to create the perfect vibe, or trying to coach friends and family who are not ever going to pay, you have to get real about where your time is going. My objective is and has been for several years, to reclaim my free time. Free time is the time you assign no monetary value to because you are not getting paid for whatever talent you are sharing with the world. I am all for going above and beyond what is required in my agreements, but I still have to establish my limits. If I don't, I will get taken advantage of every time.

B – The first bandit to eliminate is buying into the idea that the hustle and the grind are going to be what creates your success instead of focusing on the things that matter most. Staying busy is not the same thing as being successful. Keep getting rid of the hustle and embrace focused execution of the things that create revenue.

A – The second bandit is trying to be all things to all people. I keep learning this lesson over and over again. When I stay focused on the things I am best at, my work goes smoothly. When I venture off into things that I could do, but are not really in my main talent bank, I have to work significantly harder to succeed. This is not to say you shouldn't try new things. This is simply saying you need to calculate the ROI of the new things and stay focused on the ones that pay the biggest dividends.

N – Perhaps the biggest bandit of all is that of not saying no to others. I think the word "sorry" is eclipsed in difficulty by the word "no." For some reason, we find it so difficult to tell someone no when they ask for help on a fundraiser, their project, etc. This is one you will have to practice. I have filter words and rules that help me out here. If what I am being asked to help with doesn't fit with my filtered mission for the year, I need to say no. I also create rules like, "only 2 non-profit boards at a time" and "only volunteering on Saturdays." I usually respond to requests with, "I'm sorry, I have a rule that I only volunteer on Saturdays." To date, I have not been questioned for having a rule. People have just accepted it and moved on.

D – The next time bandit is doing too many things at once. When I was first in business, one of my mentors told me to finish projects before starting new ones. Do what matters most before you do what matters next most. Doing something until it is done gives you both a great feeling as well as keeping you on track. If you are trying to keep all the plates spinning on the ends of the sticks, you never get to serve dinner. You just keep spinning!

I – The next time bandit is internet surfing. I think Tim Burners-Lee was on to something when he created what we now know as the World Wide Web. It provides endless access to information. It also provides incredible distraction that can keep us from finding success at all. You will succeed at a much higher level if you limit your surfing to things related to business during business hours. Tracking your use of social media sites as well as your use of the rest of the web gives you perspective. Many people will think they have no time. Most of those same people are doing things that don't matter when they should be doing things that bring success.

T – The next time bandit is talking without limits. I think the five deadliest words in the world are "do you have a minute" because it has never meant 1 minute. Most people who ask that question really want to have 40+ minutes of your time. They only need a few minutes if they can get to the point. They use 37 minutes to keep themselves from doing work and then ask their one question and head out. They have just killed your productivity for an hour! Here is the answer I recommend to the question of whether or not you have a minute. Look at your watch, a clock, or your phone to see the time and then say, "Actually, I can give you 7 minutes right now; if you need more than that, let's schedule something for later." Most people will not want to schedule time later because they really didn't have anything important. They will either get to the point quickly, or they will say it wasn't any big deal. Either way, you just reclaimed your time.

S – The final time bandit I will talk about is shitty thinking. When we allow our minds to be cluttered, we lose track of what is important, when it is important, and why we are pursuing success. The cluttered mind is full of shit that doesn't matter. By learning to meditate for even 10 minutes in the morning, you are decluttering the pointless shit from your mind and keeping your focus on your success. If your goal is to get out of debt with direct sales and you are doing this after your regular job, you need to have a game plan for 2 hours of work after your regular work. If you will do this every single day, you will find success. Most people go into their side gig with no plan, no real goals, and only a hope that it will work. Clear the shit, the doubt, the uncertainty out of your mind, and simply act. Most of these programs have a formula you can follow to find success. Follow the damn formula!

The Wrap Up

You don't have to work more hours than everyone around you to find success. You just have to put the right work into the hours you have. The vast majority of this population will never put forth concentrated effort toward a specific end result. They have not thought things out from the end back to the beginning. Your success in this life has more to do with what you get rid of than it does with what you add in. Get rid of anything that doesn't matter and doesn't move you forward. Stay focused on what is working. Measure everything you do to ensure it is worth continuing. And finally, kick time bandits out of your life and out of your schedule!

11 Get Buzzed

Show some Attitude With Your Gratitude

One of the ideal ways to create the right core buzz in your system is to wake up to gratitude. I hear people say regularly that they are not sure they really have anything to be thankful for. These people often forget the things that have given them an advantage. They have fallen prey to the lie the world is telling them. They are not good enough. They are not successful enough. They are not good looking enough. Whatever the lie may be, it is keeping them focused on the things they don't have instead of the things they do have. It is in our haves, not our have nots that we find peace and joy and calm. My model for staying in the right buzz is to list off things I am thankful for first thing in the morning. I am thankful for my desire to write. I am thankful for my ability to type. I am thankful for my opportunity to drink coffee and share things with others. I am thankful for being healthy. I am thankful for being in control of my mental faculties. I am thankful for the chance to be thankful. If you step back from self-pity, there is always something to be thankful for. When we wrap ourselves in the "woe-is-me-blanket" of "life-suckery," we give up the buzz of awesomeness that should be our clothing for the day.

You have to embrace your badass self by being confident in what you do have instead of being whiny in what you do not have. To be fantastic in this life, you must boldly claim your awesomeness and then do something about it. The attitude part of this is what drives you to be, do, and have the life you want. If you are truly grateful for what you have, you will do something with it. If you are full of shit, you will use your whiny voice and kind of try to be thankful and then sulk back into your hole. Stand up! Stand up and thank the source of all existence for the things you already have and for the things you are about to have. Accept your current state as well as your future state of being. You are who you claim to be and who you are grateful for being. You will never be your best version if you are stuck in the quagmire of being mad about your current version. Ain't nobody got time for that kind of quagmire! This does take some concentrated effort. It takes you being willing to stand up to your own mind and wrestle it into submission. It requires you to be the master of your fate, the captain of your soul, and the confident warrior who will ride into this battle without hesitation, willing to fight as long as it takes to walk away the victor. This battle is not with another person. This battle rages within your own mind over who you are and who you are supposed to be. It is time!

Make Your Mind Or It Will Make You

In the book As A Man Thinketh, James Allen wrote, "Mind is the Master power that molds and makes, and Man is mind and evermore he takes the tool of thought, and, shaping what he wills, brings forth a thousand joys, a thousand ills: He thinks in secret and it comes to pass: Environment is but his looking-glass (Allen, 1912)." I have always loved the eloquence expressed in his writing. He was able to capture the essence of the power of our minds. We are able to bring forth a thousand joys or a thousand ills, all based on the thoughts we think on a regular basis. In the previous chapter, I had you look at your goals in a specific order. The psychological/mental goals came first because of this power that Allen spoke of so long ago. Even the Bhagavad-Gita states, "For him who has conquered the mind, the mind is the best of friends; but for the one who has failed to do so, his mind will remain the greatest enemy." Could our greatest enemy really be our minds? I absolutely believe that! I have spoken with hundreds of entrepreneurs over the last two decades who each have a demon that chases them. For some, they refer to it as their "asshole self." For others, it is the "black dog." For still others, they simply call it "the darkness," with a few people seeing this struggle as a "dragon" at the mouth of the cave of greatness, ready to destroy them. No matter what it is referred to, it is still made up of that portion of the mind that brings criticism and self-doubt. In my book 6 Demons of

Fear, this was the first demon I wrote about. I wrote about it first because it is the roughest of the demons for a human to face. To kick its ass, you must first exercise control over your own power of mind.

To make your mind your bitch, you must learn the warning signs of your mind going down the dark road of destruction. What are the questions you are asking yourself that lead to you doubting your greatness or questioning your worth? My questions center around whether or not I am good enough, really good enough to do the things I do. This is objectively humorous, since I have been successful for years at training, coaching, writing, and developing the potential of others. Subjectively (emotionally), that dark matter in my brain will bring up any time I have failed in the past. It will bring up any time I did not meet or exceed expectations. And, it will bring up the idea that the rug is about to be pulled out from under me. When I speak to a group of 200 executives, it will center in on the one person who did not like what I had to say and forget about the 199 that loved everything I said. It is the focus area that matters in the end. I am not that unlike other entrepreneurs. The key is to learn to give a shit only about the things that move us forward and to not give a shit about the things that hold us back. When we master this mental shift, we find peace as well as our ability to bring forth a thousand joys and zero ills.

This shift is 3 a step process. You have to HIT the dark matter of your brain as hard as you can daily, and you will make it your bitch.

- H – Hold yourself as if you were physically happy. Even when you do not feel happy, you move your body to reflect what you would look like if you were in a happy state. Smile while looking at yourself in a mirror for 2 minutes and see what a difference it begins to make. Hold your body posture, your face, and your entire being as if you were happy. Your physiology controls the electrical impulses to the brain, which control the chemical production in your brain, which controls the hormonal release in the brain. This means… you can control the factory output of happy drugs in the mind by setting the factory of your body up correctly.
- I – Intentions create actions. We must intend to be happy on a daily basis. We must intend to feel successful. We must set our intentions to be reflected in our daily affirmations and our daily actions. People often go through life with no intentions in any direction. This keeps them from experiencing the joy, love, security, and happiness waiting for them. Your mind will either make you its bitch, or you will make your mind your bitch. You have to intend to be the victor in order to be the victor in this battle.
- T – Take action every single day! It is in motion that we achieve motivation. It is not in feeling alone! When we take deliberate action toward our goals, regardless of our feelings, our feelings and psychological well-being will catch up. I have found that exercise helps me maintain right action in

other areas as well. When I exercise, I stimulate the motivational components of the brain, create endorphins, and get the chance to embrace the happiness drugs my own mind can create. The pre-frontal cortex of the human mind allows us to override our feeling state. This is the fundamental difference between humans and the rest of the animal world. When we stay in motion, we can make feelings secondary. In taking deliberate action and staying in motion, both our thoughts and feelings move forward in harmony toward our end goal. In this manner, the mind works for us instead of against us.

It's not me, it's you, breaking up with your past

There are only two days in our life that we are incapable of changing in any way: yesterday and tomorrow. "Do you have any idea what I used to be like?" I have been asked this question by people trying to figure out success over and over again. They stay stuck in the world that used to exist instead of living in the world of the present. When we focus on the way things were, we lose sight of the way things can be. I have not gone back to the class reunions for the small Texas town I grew up in for one main reason. The version of me that existed during that time does not exist anymore. Many of the people I knew from high school seem to still wish they were back in high school. Those were their glory days, and they still miss them and long to get them back. It isn't that I did not have fun growing up. In fact, I had a great experience of growing up and enjoyed my time in that small town as well as in the larger town I moved to as a sophomore. Without naming the towns, I moved from C-town to A-town at 15 years old. I remember the day my father sat my brothers and me down and asked us what we thought of the opportunity to move to a larger town. I remember immediately thinking it sounded like a great idea. My dad was great at fixing groups of people, and that group of people needed fixin'.

I remember thinking about how I could be anyone I wanted to be in this new town. Nobody knew me. Nobody had a preconceived notion of who I was. Nobody would try to pigeon-hole me into being who I was in 3rd grade. So, I went to work creating the new me in the weeks leading up to the move. I planned out how I would talk, how I would carry myself, how I would dress, and how I would be perceived. When we made the move, I played the part. I was very happy with how easy it was to be seen as a new person and really kind of amazed that I had not tried to reinvent myself sooner, even without a move. The lesson I learned at 15 years old was invaluable in my journey for the rest of my life. I can be anyone I want to be. I simply have to believe I am that person in my mind and act as if. At the same time, I do have to let go of who I was. I cannot be two people, well, not without needing medication and a bit of therapy. I can be a new person anytime I want to be, however. If I can change who I am, you can too! I have gone through this transformation several times over the years. When a version of me seems to become stale or stops moving forward in life, I simply map out who I am going to be, let go of who I was, and act as if I already am the person I have created.

Letting go of the past means letting go of past hurts, past descriptors, past limiters, past weaknesses, and anything that would drag you back into the old version of yourself. It does not mean that you burn your old pictures, get rid of anyone you knew during that time, or even that you have to move out of the area. You simply have to see you as the new you. Your new truth about yourself has to be the actual truth about yourself. Let go of everything that held you back in the past. Use self-suggestion to reinforce your new description of who you are. Don't act in the way you would have before. Act in the way you are now. Believe it. Think it. Do it. Achieve it. You've got this!

Stay Buzzed… One way or another

Meditate on a regular basis and keep the vision of the real you in front of you at all times. In chapter 2, in the section called "This is your brain," I described a simple process of meditating. You have alternatives if you feel that holding an image and focusing on a new version of reality are not your thing. You can also journal. I started journaling when I was young, gave it up, and then picked it up again about a year ago. The process of journaling focuses primarily on having a conversation with the two sides of yourself. You will have a weak and a strong self, a yin and a yang.

In Chinese philosophy, yin and yang represent darkness/bad and light/good. Within each of the sides, a piece of the other must necessarily exist in order to achieve balance. One cannot exist without the other. We spend way too much time trying to get rid of darkness altogether instead of realizing it is what creates the differentiation of light. If all was light, we would not know darkness. Without darkness, we would not know light. As you journal, embrace both sides of self. They are both a part of who you are, and both provide insight into your future and your success. When I journal, I allow both to have a voice. To me, light is the voice of reason, peace, and calmness. Darkness is the voice of emotion without reason. Light is long-term success. Darkness is considering only the here and now. Light is my future. Darkness is my past.

My conversation with self focuses on finding the right path to success both in that moment and in the future. When I go back and forth with myself, I am able to overcome the shit holding me back, throwing darts at my self-confidence, and trying to keep me from a brighter future. I have to have this conversation! It is what allows me to see what is really going on in my head. When I am able to work through the full conversation, I get out of victim mode and fully own my next steps toward success. This is a form of meditating through an issue. It doesn't involve a trance, progressive relaxation, or sitting in any given position. It simply involves a prayer-like state where I give up the external voices and live into the two voices in my head. I would encourage you to talk with yourself in a journaling experiment. Ask yourself questions. Give yourself answers. Keep writing until you uncover the light in the darkness, the yang in the yin. You will be amazed at how well this works to get you through your challenges.

This shit works… But only if you work it!

I have sat back and looked at the roughly 30-45 minutes per day it would require to do all of the work on self and thought, "I don't have the time." When I do have this thought, I start the conversation with self (journaling) in order to discover if it is time or desire that is missing. So far, it has always been the desire to actually move myself forward that was missing. Even though it sounds crazy to think about not desiring to move forward, many of us get caught up in wallowing in our own bullshit because it is safe. We hold ourselves back in order to keep our story of victimhood alive. I have heard the following statements from people I have coached over the years…

- Every time I get close to success, something happens, and it all goes away.
- No matter what I do, I can't seem to succeed.
- I have tried everything, and nothing works.
- People in this town just don't like me. They always find a way to knock me back on my ass.
- You don't understand what it is like to struggle.

- I am just doomed to suffer my whole life.
- I am struggling, but I am okay with it because I would never want to be like one of those rich assholes.

When our story is more important than our success, we will stay stuck in the story instead of moving forward. If you will read and re-read this book and apply the lessons I am teaching you, you will find success. I heard a statement by Jen Sincero a few weeks ago that less than 5% of people do anything different after going through a program. She said this included going through the really expensive programs. The problem is not whether or not there is good information out there. The problem we are facing is whether or not we are willing change ourselves. Most people want to change their circumstances… as long as they don't have to do any work on themselves. That isn't the way life works! You have to change you so that your circumstances will change. Whining about the shit going wrong in your life is pointless. It doesn't change anything for the better.

If you are willing to apply the information you have learned, your life will necessarily change. Facing struggles is supposed to sharpen us, mold us, build us into a better version of ourselves. If you face a struggle but don't learn a lesson, you will simply get knocked on your ass every time a challenge comes your way. Who you become on your journey of success is more valuable than what you face or even what you overcome. This shit works if you work. If you don't do anything different, you will not get any different results. Just reading a book without applying the information obtained is like buying a diet book but not doing anything recommended. You will not lose weight by simply owning the formula. You have to apply the lessons! Since I began writing the formula, I have sold out all of my training days for the next year. I have not done that before. This is multiple six figures of work booked more than a year out. I am not saying that to brag. I am saying that to make sure you understand. What you work will work for you. Go work the system so that the system can bring you the success you desire!

I need nothing. I have everything.

We walk through life wondering whether or not we are good enough. We wonder what others will think of us. I want to say this as clearly as possible. When we see ourselves needing something else before being accepted by ourselves, we feel inadequate. When we feel inadequate, we do not perform at our best. You will get better each day **unless** you see yourself as inadequate or lacking. Giving up the need for validation allows you to become authentic in your success. Clinging to your need for approval pushes you to make decisions that are not in alignment with your highest self.

When someone asks me who they need to be in order to be successful, they are asking if they need to give up on themselves. NO! You don't give up on you. Instead, you embrace who you are. Find a way to leverage your gifts, your knowledge, your expertise, all of who you are in order to be successful. Make a list of everything you have as an asset. Can you read, write, speak, walk, talk, travel, smile, teach, or do anything else? If so, you are at an advantage over many of the most successful people in the world. Nick Vujicic was born with no arms and no legs. In his inspirational story, he talks about how he was so depressed in high school because of being so different. He felt helpless for the longest time. His janitor knew that he was a Christian and encouraged him over and over again to talk to the Fellowship of Christian Athletes about his story. When he finally did talk about how each person should love themselves and accept the love of God, multiple students cried. He recounts how shocked he was at the overwhelmingly positive response. He said he was even more shocked to learn that even the beautiful young ladies in the room felt inadequate. It was that short speech that launched him toward a professional speaking career and the start of his organization called Life Without Limbs. What is fantastic to me is that Nick has made something incredible of himself without any excuses. What is, perhaps, even more fantastic is the fact that a high school janitor used his gifts of observation, encouragement, and influence to help a depressed young man realize he had a lot to offer this world. The ripple effect of the encouragement of that one janitor has changed thousands of lives. When one person uses their gifts, it prompts the next and the next and the next to fully express their gifts as well. If you want to learn more about Nick, you can go to www.lifewithoutlimbs.org. What if Nick would have never spoken to a group of fellow students? What if he had never started speaking around the world to encourage young people to believe in themselves regardless of their struggles? What if the janitor had not seen the potential in him? The what ifs can go on and on, but so can the ripples of impact made every single day. Your gifts and talents and effort are needed in this world. Don't ever forget that! You have something to offer this world that only you can offer! So, start with who you are and where you are. Dive into life with a vigor that propels you toward success, and never back down! Nick had the ability to speak as a 14-year-old. He could not walk on his own or pick anything up on his own, but he could think and speak and observe and encourage. There is something awesome in each one of us!

AA Forever - Always Awesome

You have to see the best version of you as if you are already that version. We don't become what we hope to one day be. We become what we accept that we already are. Every single day, you have to wake up and see the awesome in the mirror. This means being grateful for the gifts and talents in your life and being determined to acquire more of them. You are an ever-evolving being. Whether you want to or not, you are going to be different today than you were yesterday. You are going to grow and change and reshape. When you change beliefs, you literally begin to reshape the structure of your face. In my book, Faces of Reality, I describe how you read a person based on their facial structure. One of the most fascinating aspects of physiognomy, the science behind face reading, is that your face shifts when you shift your mind. According to Universe Today, an atom is made up of protons, neutrons, and electrons. You probably recall this from junior high science class. Inside of those subatomic components are quarks, leptons, and bosons. Inside of those sub-subatomic particles are simply trace energy. It is still one positive charge, one negative charge, and one neutral charge. I believe there is a positive path, a negative path, and you, the neutral. The neutral component of matter is what determines what matter will be presented to the world. Your pressure is what must be applied in order to shift the reality in which you exist. Trace energy is nothingness, and out of nothingness, existence is created. The book in your hands, or the audio program you are listening to right now began from nothing. It took the right pressure to shift it into something that could be used to reshape reality for everyone reading it or listening to it.

The acorn holds the oak in waiting. The acorn must be buried under the pressure of the earth, have rain and soil, sun and wind, and struggle in order to grow into a mighty oak. Without the struggle, without the breakthrough, the acorn stays only as potential. It never becomes the oak it was meant to be. As it begins to take root and grow, other trees might look at it and think, you should be a pine, or a fir, or something else. They may tell the oak it is not needed or not worthwhile. Does the oak bend to the will of the other trees? NO! The oak remains true to itself. It knows the potential inside and grows to the tallest, most glorious version of itself possible. It does not stop growing because others are intimidated by its growth and success. It grows because that is what the energy inside it was meant to do. What is inside of you? What greatness has lay dormant, waiting for the right struggle, the right pressure, the right conditions to reveal itself? You see, inside every struggle lies the seed of an equivalent or greater benefit. Stop looking at the struggle and start looking at the benefit intended for you. Stop looking at the setback and start looking at the setup for your success. Be the oak inside of you. Begin from the place you are, and never look back!

Mic Drop

"Life is a daring adventure or nothing." --Helen Keller. You are who you are and where you are because you have chosen to be who and where you are. This may suck if you are not in a position of success yet, and it may be awesome if you are. You have to accept full responsibility for yourself, your successes, your failures, and all of your choices leading up to this point. Believing in an internal locus of control, according to psychology, is one of, if not the only, predicter of success in your life. You are either in charge of you or the world is in charge of you. Which is it? Please initial your choice.

___________I am in charge of me!
___________The world is in charge of me!

Take a moment and think about who you are. You are on stage. This is the performance of your life. This is it. There is no backing out now! As you start to speak, you either project greatness out from the stage to the audience or you wait to see what others say and then you repeat it. When you are waiting on the world to dictate who you are, you never find the potential inside of you. You have to speak, then adjust, then speak, then adjust, then speak, and so on. You are in charge of what happens next, at every next that comes up. You may not be able to control the circumstances around you, but you can control you in the middle of the circumstances. You can determine what you will do next when something bad happens or when something good happens. If you practice this internal locus of control and fully accept that you are the only one responsible for you, then the next chapter becomes easy. Then, you will truly own your shit as well as your glory.

12 Own Your Shit

This chapter will be on how you take the information and maximize personal engagement on a daily basis. Your personal engagement is measured by your capacity to choose your own path. One of the most impactful principles in psychology is the Locus of Control Theory. This theory states that we will look at the things in our life as either internally or externally controlled. An internal locus of control indicates I am in control of the next move I make with anything I face. If something goes wrong, I take control of how I view it and what I do next about it. If the economy throws me a curve ball, I adjust my swing and still knock it out of the park. An external locus of control indicates I am not in control of what happens in my life. With this side of the theory, I am controlled by my circumstances and my environment. When the world throws me a curve ball, I make an excuse as to why I wasn't able to hit it out of the park.

I think this principle of owning your shit, all of it, and not making any excuses, is the most powerful tool we have in creating our path to success. The moment you own that you are who you are and where you are because you made a series of decisions that led you to this point, that is the day you get to decide on any point you wish to reach in the future. You have to have this starting point. Without it, your goals, plans, and strategies (GPS) will not take you anywhere. Make a list of the excuses you have used to keep you where you are, and then state at least one thing wrong with each of them.

My Excuses And Why They Are B.S.

Excuse	It is B.S. because…

Strip It Down

The concept of living an essentialist life, especially in business, is one of the most profound ideas I have been exposed to in the last 5 years. By stripping away the things that do not bring us joy, success, fulfillment, and the money we are seeking, we are better able to keep our MOJO. Many of the excuses people use are there as crutches. They are the busy pursuits of our life that allow us to say we don't have the time, energy, or ability to go after our dreams. Getting rid of the things outside of the dream path will allow you to push full steam ahead toward the destination you know was intended for you. You just went through your excuses and why they were no good, which means you know why they must go. Now, let's focus on how you plan what is allowed into your time. You will have a Key 3 for your day. For most people, this Key 3 will be the same today, tomorrow, and from now on. For a few people, it may shift, but most people are consistent in this one. These are the key 3 focus areas for you to be successful in your job. For example, I have to grow my own potential, invest in the potential of others, and bill somebody for the investment. If I do these three things every single work-day, I am a huge success. If I allow myself to start with things outside of my key 3, I will likely struggle to ever have time for those things. Starting with what is key enables you to end your day with a sense of accomplishment. What are the broad brushstrokes of things that truly matter for you in the work you are doing?

Key 1	Key 2	Key 3

Heavy Breathing Leads To Success

Learning to breathe properly will help to oxygenate your brain and put you on the path to greater productivity. Your personal engagement requires you to be healthy and connected. You will have to be willing to expand your lungs as well as your mind. Think of the lungs as being divided into thirds. Most people breathe with the top of their lungs which gives them enough oxygen to keep moving, but it never fully oxygenates the body. The way we sit, stand, and carry ourselves will have an impact on the brain itself. The brain needs oxygen to function. In fact, it needs a good deal of oxygen. The following three illustrations demonstrate ways in which you can bring oxygen to each of the parts of the lungs. You may not want to do them with your door open at work, or even at a local restaurant. I only say this because of the looks I have gotten when trying to effectively breathe in a restaurant in the airport. You will, however, want to spend time breathing into each part of your lungs on a daily basis.

Position 1 is the top of the lungs. Rest your hands on your lap, palms down, in a comfortable position. Hold your back straight, sitting either on your knees or sitting up in a chair. When you breathe in, focus on filling the top of your lungs and expanding your upper chest during each breath. Breathe in through your nose and out through your mouth, creating a circular motion with the air.

Position 2 is the center portion of your lungs. This is where you pull your hands up close to your armpits, palms down with your fingertips facing one another or pointing toward one another. Hold your back straight and either sit on your knees or sit up straight in a chair. Focus on filling the center of your upper body with air. You should feel the lower portion of the rib cage expanding, just above the abdomen area.

Position 3 is the lower portion of the lungs. This is the most often neglected area of the lungs for those who are not singers or athletes. The older we get, the more we breathe shallow, or at the top of the lung. Your capacity to oxygenate your body depends on hitting this portion of the lungs on a regular basis. Raise your arms above your head, then fold your arms down and backwards, placing the palms on the upper center of your back. Try to keep your elbows close to the sides of your head. This narrows the upper body and makes breathing down into the abdomen area more natural. Breathe in deeply through your nose, expanding your belly on each in-breath, holding the air for a 3 count and letting the air out for a 5 count, through your mouth.

You can determine how many breaths you would like to take. My focus is generally 10 slow breaths in each position, beginning with position 1 and going through position 3. The entire process only takes about 5 minutes and gives your body and brain much more oxygen than it had without the breathing. We are called on to solve problems, fix challenges, and build the potential and energy of others. This is only possible if you have something to offer. Breathing gives you the mental and physical capacity to share energy and multiply energy in others. If you will do this breathing exercise before you leave the house in the morning, even if you only do a few breaths in each position, you will have more energy to start your day and will achieve a greater level of focus. Breath is the beginning of momentum. Don't skip over this! You will need the extra potential energy in order to move others toward right action, which brings us next to mojo.

MOJO

Mojo goes beyond your ability to turn into *Austin Powers* and pick up a hot date. It really ties into a combination of three things: your directed confidence in self, your directed external awareness, and your directed enthusiasm. En-Theos, or from God, is the origin of the word enthusiasm. Without a focus, though, your enthusiasm is pointless, no matter where it comes from. Your confidence in yourself is pointless as well unless you are aware of where to focus it. Directed self-confidence is your ability to believe in yourself completely when it ties to a related objective. Think of this as a burning desire for success that you are so confident you are able to attain that you can let go of any worry, any stress, any doubt of its attainment. You believe in your ability so completely that you let go of chasing the goal because you know it is already yours as soon as the time is right. External awareness is one's attunement to the opportunities surrounding them. When you are able to spend time visualizing the possession of your desires, your mind begins to see this new truth. The new truth is that God or the universe (use whichever term suits you best for the energy that makes up all existence) is arranging things on your behalf. It is setting up your success for you. All you have to do is pay attention to the signs and act when the opportunity is presented to you. Finally, one must act with enthusiasm. It is fairly easy to distinguish between manufactured enthusiasm and faith-backed enthusiasm. If you accept the gifts of the universe, the coincidences, and the divine intervention, your ability to be excited is genuine. You are truly grateful for what is being given to you and, at the same time, you fully expected it to happen. You are wrapping yourself en-theos, in God's desire for your success. If you do this, how can you lose? Mojo applies to any targeted goal one would have in life. It can be used for good, or it can be used for evil. My hope is that you use it for accomplishing greatness in this life.

When you embrace these three components of mojo, your goals become your primary focus in life. You can have goals related to different areas, just like we discussed earlier in this book, but each goal must be backed by your mojo. Another way to look at MOJO would be to use an acronym: Mental acumen, Outward mindset, Juiced up expression, and Opportunity-based awareness.

- Mental acumen is your development of skills in your specialized focus area of success. When you invest time in your development regularly, success becomes easier and easier. Every time you add a tool to your toolbox, you build your ease of success. This is where reading books, developing self, and expanding your skills becomes a critical aspect of growth. Your Mental acumen is being tuned in to the right things in order to allow the right opportunities to appear.

- Having an outward mindset keeps your focus on what others are doing, how they are reacting to you, and what matters the most to them in their interaction with you. It has been my experience that others will always show you what they are thinking and feeling before they will tell you. They show their internal world through expression in their external world. In my book Faces of Reality, I describe the psychological makeup of a person based on the physical structure of their face. When you tune in to a person, you learn how to adapt to exactly what they are needing from you at any given point. If you couple face reading with the reading of body language and micro-expressions (subtle expressions in reaction to what you are saying or doing), you can know a person deeper than they know themselves. If you are only focused on what you are going to say, you will miss out on knowing how you need to say what you are saying. Stay focused on others before you create your expression of self.
- You have to juice up your manner of presenting information in order to inspire great responses from others. Enthusiasm, or juiced up expression, is

one of the most critical things you possess. Enthusiasm has always been and will always be contagious. We both influence and move others with our excitement about a goal. When I was first in business, I was so excited about what I was offering that I had people call the office after giving me a check to ask what they bought. They were very excited, just not fully aware. I have significantly increased my communication clarity without giving up the enthusiasm. This pulls people along like the wake of a boat pulls anything behind it. Get excited about your future! Get excited about your present. Just get freakin' excited! Focus that energy towards the engagement of self and then others in the attainment of your goals.

- Opportunity-based awareness is learning to tune in to the things going on around you. I wanted to be tuned into money as a young person, so I began focusing on seeing money everywhere. I have found pennies, nickels, dimes, quarters, and all ranges of dollars up to hundreds, just waiting for me. The more you tune in to the frequency of success, the more it tunes in to you. If you hate rich people, you will not be one of them. You have to love people, all people. You have to embrace the brilliance of people who have already attained the things you desire. Your attitude about opportunities

> and success will determine whether or not those things chase you down. If your attitude is negative and judgmental, they will run from you. If you hate money and then tell it you really want it around, that makes you a shitty friend to money. Your significant other wouldn't stick around for that bullshit, why would success or money?

When Would Now Be A Good Time?

You have to have a quick response rule, a mantra, a battle cry, or something that gets your ass out of bed and moves you toward success. One of the questions I ask myself when wondering when a good time would be to make a positive change is... When would now be a good time to make that change? By triggering my mind that it is time to move forward, I position myself for success. I think back to when I was in high school and trying to motivate myself to get up at 4:30 in the morning to go to the gym. I would wake up, look at the clock, think about not going to bed until 1, then start to think about going back to sleep. I was a bit harsh with myself, but I had to jolt my system to get into gear. I would say, "GO! Now!" My goal was to stop thinking and start acting. It is overthinking that creates writer's block, flabby stomachs, the avoidance of success, and a host of other rash-like irritants.

Whatever your tactic may be, you need a tactic. You need to have a plan for when your mind gets in the way of your action. Desire without action produces nothing! I remember a guy who wanted to start a consulting business back when I had only been in business for about a year. He thought about it, prayed over it, and thought about it more. Every day, he focused on sending out positive vibes and trusting that success would find him. He stayed in business until he ran out of money, never having closed a single deal. Success is not difficult, but it is action-based. If you are unwilling to take action, you are unwilling to succeed. I get so damn frustrated with people who have all of the talent required to succeed and none of the action. Here are a few of the mantras that have worked for me, my coaching clients, and one big-time author…

- Mel Robbins (big-time author): The 5-Second Rule… when you are faced with a decision to act toward your success or not, count down from 5 to 1 and blast off your ass and get something done.
- Construction Client: *I take action. I don't wait for inaction to take me.* This is the phrase he says every time he thinks about not doing the bid, not following up with the prospect, or not getting his crew to work.
- Author/Speaker: *GSD Baby!* Get Shit Done is the mantra of those who are compelled to act and act assertively in the direction of success.
- National Account Manager: *Keep it simple stupid!* When he begins to overthink things, he reminds himself that success is easy when you are in motion.

May I Have Another?

Newton's First Law of Motion states that a body at rest will remain at rest unless an outside force acts on it, and a body in motion at a constant velocity will remain in motion in a straight line unless acted upon by an outside force. When you begin your success journey, you start as the body at rest. Your conscious choices, what you read, what you listen to, the seminars you attend, each of these acts is the outside force acting in conjunction with your thoughts to move you toward a new destination. Once you are in motion, your best bet is to stay in motion, maintaining a focus on your end goal. Along the way, it is likely you will have multiple outside forces acting to deviate you from your course. The more focused you are and the more velocity you attain, the less likely one of those objects or people will sway you from your course. There is no greater time to win than when you have already had a win. I see too many entrepreneurs decide to rest on their laurels (different word for asses) when they have just done something worthwhile. If you have achieved something of significance, take massive and directed action to achieve something else of significance. Don’t step back from your accomplishment and try to stay in your comfort zone of success. Instead, maintain a focus on the directed actions you can control. A body of failure tends to remain in failure until acted upon by a positive inside force, and a success in motion tends to stay in the motion of success until acted upon by a negative inside force. (Jody’s Law of Success Motion)

"Every action and feeling is preceded by a thought." James Allen

Your success or failure is determined by the thoughts you think. You will have a residual image of self that places you into a specific success zone or failure zone. What do you think the difference is between someone who is succeeding in the area you are focused on and someone who is not? Is it their good looks? Is it their parents? Is it their neighborhood? The answer to each of these questions is a resounding NOPE! The difference between the person in your industry at the top and the person at the bottom is the makeup of their thoughts. Think of what you look like as the top producer in your area. It doesn't matter if you are in network marketing, have started your own service business, or sell physical products. Your success has almost nothing to do with the product itself. It has everything to do with who you are from the inside out. Your mind is your product, your service, and your reputation. See the perfect version of you every single day. See it, embrace it, believe it, and live into it. See yourself as the person who takes massive directed action toward success because that is what top performers do. When you embrace the image and it becomes real to you, you must overlay your residual self-image into reality. This is when reality bends in your favor. There is no greater time to sell than when you have just closed a deal. There is no greater time to deal with a challenge than when you have just dealt with a challenge. Your drive to succeed and to energize yourself is the result of capitalizing on momentum.

Attraction Matters

We have to position ourselves to attract business. We must present ourselves with some level of expertise and some ability to eliminate the problems that another person might be having. If you can solve a problem, you can attract more opportunities to get paid to solve a problem. Some of the best advice I was given was to identify a problem that kept executives up at night, and then create a solution for that specific problem. We will always pay more to eliminate a problem than to gain an opportunity. I can prove this to you by you answering two simple questions. Would you be willing to work for me for one hour for $5? Most people would say no because they are already getting more than $5 per hour. Second question… would you spend an hour looking for a $5 item you lost? Most people would say yes to this one because we lost an item and want it back. We pay more to eliminate loss than to create gain.

I have been in the training and speaking business for a couple of decades now, as I am writing this book. One of the great lessons I learned early in my career is that people want work with someone that is busy more than with someone who has nothing to do. They assume that because the person is always on the go, they are already successful. We desire to be around the best. When I began indicating how busy I was, I became more rare of a commodity and was therefore more sought after. At the writing of this book, I am sold out on available weekdays for speaking/training for the next 12 ½ months. Because I am sold out so far in advance, I am able to book higher priced gigs a year out than I would have been able to book a month out. Even when I was not this busy, I would make it a point to indicate I had to check my calendar to see if I had the time to do the work I was being asked about. There were times I had nothing on my schedule for the next 8 days, and knew it, but I still acted like I was highly sought after and would have to get back with the potential customer about their requested dates and times. I made it a point to not have a lot of time to hang out after a presentation as well. Indicating the need to rush off helped to position me in the minds of others as a sought-after speaker. There are other things I have done as well to become more attractive in the marketplace.

Carry yourself in the image you wish for others to have of you. The manner in which a person carries themselves is based on several factors. Dress or clothing is one of the factors, but it is not the only factor. When we carry ourselves in order to create a specific image, we must be high in external awareness. This means you are continuously reading others in order to know what they are thinking, not just what they are saying. It is tempting to live into someone else's model, but it is also a fatal flaw. You can model the success behaviors of another person, but you need to create your image from the inside out in order for it to last. If you are not getting others to respond to you based on your current image, experiment with other ways to carry yourself until you find the one that works. The quality of your communication is measured solely by the quality of the response you receive from others. Your image is the communication of who you are. If your response is bad, look within before you look without.

Your ability to be pleasing to be around rests with your ability to connect with others. If you are constantly projecting without ever considering the needs of others, you are not effective in your communication. Many people think they are great communicators because they push hard, close hard, or demand attention. This is not the case. You are a great communicator only when you both understand and master the entire circle of communication. There is a sender, a message, encoding in the message, a medium for the transfer of the message, a receiver, decoding and interpretation of the message, a response (verbal and non-verbal), and a reverse of the process back to the original sender. Our perceptual filters often get in the way of the clarity of the messaging. Paralanguage accounts for the manner in which we are interpreted as we speak. It is the pitch, tone, pace, and projection of your voice along with your body language and facial expression. Personal appearance is the aspect of communication that impacts the validity of the message before the message is delivered. I have an entire course on these aspects of communicating that dive into creating a deliberate image. Take some time to learn what others are interpreting and get out of your own way in the process. Don't be so hung up on one idea that you are unwilling to listen to multiple angles in finding success. When you are open to doing what works instead of being set on being right, success becomes much more likely. In other words, you can either be right or you can be rich, but you will have to make a choice. In your choice, you are determining if you will be the person the world needs and will rewards or if you are going to simply be who you want to be regardless of meeting the needs of the world around you. Neither is wrong, but they are rewarded at a much different level. Choose wisely!

13 Lucky 13 – The Wrap Up

This final chapter is a quick review of the steps required for you to succeed in life. It is a way to summarize the points, keep you on track, and give you something to look at as a review. I have long been told that we should believe in superstition and should have lucky signs. 13 is often considered one of those unlucky numbers, which is why I think we should flip it the bird, stomp it down, and show that we are in charge, not some damn number. Let's dive into what you must do every single day in order to have the success you desire and live into your highest potential.

Be Intentional About Your Belief System

Your success, your failure, your strategy, your entire being, each of these is the result of your belief about self. Too many people go through life believing what the rest of the world says about them. They believe their worth is based on their grades, or their last performance review. They give up on their dreams because someone tells them they are out of their reach. They walk through life avoiding right action because they don't believe they are worthy of the success. Your mantra moving forward should be…

In the past, I have not done what was right because I have not believed in myself in the right way. I will no longer accept less than the greatness I desire. I am intentional every single day about who I am. I am a success! I am offered advantages at every turn. I am continuously placed in the pathway of opportunity. I am all that I need to be, and I am desired by all that I encounter. I believe in myself, and I believe in the greatness of those around me. I am excited, driven, fun, cooperative, inspired, and I always finish on top!

Be Intentional About Your Self-Projection

Too often, people walk through life oblivious to the impact they are having on others. They do and say things to drive people crazy because they are weak and unsure of themselves. Too many people believe that things are not about them. They fail because they think the world is always about someone else. It is not! Your mantra moving forward should be…

I am fully conscious of the impact I have on the world around me by accepting the truth about myself. When I am honest about myself and I embrace the image and the magnetic field I am projecting into the world, I am in control of my present as well as my future. I am the kind of person who sends love into the world and not judgement. I am the kind of person who others long to be around because I am fully accepting of them. I am this way because I am fully accepting of myself and my personal responsibility for my own success. I am not waiting on anyone to turn me into a success. I am a success! I am intentional about knowing myself and believing in my potential.

Believe In Yourself Even In The Face Of Your Enemy

The battle inside of you, and never the battle outside of you, is the only thing capable of holding you back. We have each seen the devil of failure in our lives, and he looks very much like the person in the mirror. Too many people in this world refuse to enter the arena and face the giant. You are no longer one of those people. Your mantra moving forward should be…

No longer do I cower in fear of either failure or success. Rather, I step boldly into the arena, ready to fight for what is rightfully mine. I am willing to suffer the blows required in order to stand proudly over my enemy. I will change when required, discipline myself daily, and act in accordance with my desired outcome. I realize that I can only win the fight if I am willing to take the hits. I am willing. I desire to hit the struggle head on and kick its ass! I am a warrior, and I act even when I am afraid. I will never back down! I will fight until I succeed. I am the great warrior in the arena of life and business, and I cannot be beaten because I will not quit. I am the success I desire, and I will accept nothing less!

Have A Fundamental Understanding Of What Holds You Back And Propels You Forward

Many people are afraid of the work required to be a success. They are afraid to face their demons of doubt and self-criticism. They are afraid to let go of their desire to be liked by those who care nothing for their success. You are not that person. You seek out understanding and wisdom. You are willing to fail because it will take you one step closer to success. You are willing to change yourself in the face of any circumstance. Many people seek only ways to change the world around them. You are different. Your mantra should be…

I accept who I am and work daily to become the highest version of myself. I act when others hesitate. I seek out the deepest parts of myself to expose the demons of doubt holding me back, and I destroy them in a flash. I read and study every day. I learn all that I can so that I have more to offer today than I did yesterday. I learn from the greats as well as from the failures in my area. I learn what to do, what not to do, what to believe about myself, and what to give up. I understand that I must change myself in order to change my circumstances, and I am unafraid!

Up Your Leadership Game With Self And Others

To lead is to influence. Far too many people in this world think that leadership is just about a title or a position. They think that being a leader is about money and power. It is not. It is about personal growth and the growth of influence. You will not back down from leading yourself so that you may lead others. You will lead yourself to greatness by learning the principles of greatness, the principles of self-discipline, and the principles of right thought. You will use what you learn to inspire a new generation of greatness in others with all that you do. Your mantra will be…

I embody a great leader because I am humble yet confident, patient yet driven, open to growth yet determined. I am a great leader because I have mastered my mind and my mind determines my greatness. I use all that I know in order to attain greater wisdom and build a better world for myself and others. I lead because I have chosen to be a leader. I lead because I have influence with myself and others. I invest in my leadership ability, and my team follows me, is inspired by me, and desires to see me succeed, just as I desire to see them succeed! I am a leader!

Clearly Define Your Values, Actions, Results And Self

Far too many people have given up on living an ethical life. They take actions that would create mistrust instead of trust. They achieve results that are inadequate and seek ways to push their failures off on others. They are weak because they lack a model for living a strong life. They lack the ability to make solid decisions in the face of challenging odds. That is not you. You are different. You are driven by values. Your mantra moving forward will be…

I know my values, and they guide my every belief, thought, action, and result. I am intentional about the values that guide me, and I am unwavering in my commitment to be a person of values. Every action I take, every behavior I exhibit, makes my values unmistakable to the world around me. I would rather live by strong principles than easy money. I am in this for the long haul. I am committed to achieving the results I desire because I am driven by the right values. I cannot help but be a light in a world of darkness because my values create the brightness of my action. I cannot help but achieve success because I take right action every single day. My success is therefore predictable. I am the sum total of my values. I am a winner because winners bring others along with them. I am a person of values. I am a person of action. I am a person of success! I AM!

Create Your Culture And Business On Purpose

Everything in your life will either be the result of you choosing to be in control of the outcomes or choosing to not be in control of the outcomes. Make no mistake, you are making a choice! The culture of your organization is the personality of the company. Your employees will judge the company and determine what value you see in them as a part of the company. When they are making this judgment call, they are determining the amount of discretionary effort to put forth. They are not just looking at how fun it will be to work for you and the organization.

Whether you have just you, one employee, or hundreds, it is critical to create your organizational personality on purpose. The number one reason a customer decides to stop doing business with your organization is because of a bad service experience. LogMeIn indicates in their research that 76% of the reason people will stop doing business with you can be traced back to this one thing (O'Donnell, 2015). Why is it that a company would provide bad service? The reality is that it is often an encounter with either a small handful of employees or even a single employee that creates the negative image in the mind of the customer. So, why would an employee or small group of employees feel it is okay to mistreat a customer? They often feel this way because their supervisor or up has mistreated them or has not been intentional about investing positive energy in them. This happens when a company is not intentional about creating the right culture. We often hear that the customer is 1st. This is a load of crap. If the customer is first, we often feel justified in mistreating our people. The paradigm shift required to have a great culture is that of seeing the employee as more first than the customer. They are both important! However, if we don't treat our people great, they will not have the positive emotional capital required to treat our customers great. Be intentional in your creation of the right culture and the right business.

Step back from your business and from your ego and seek out a new truth. You will be as successful as the people are in your organization. In order to push your organization forward, your people have to trust you as their leader. They have to trust the organization and its intent, or mission. When we are not purposeful in how we lead, we are purposely choosing to mislead our people. I want to make sure to drill the point in as strongly as possible. Your organizational culture, your success, your teams are only as good as you are. You must continuously invest in yourself as well as purposefully building your brand from the inside out. Treat your employees as if they are volunteers and can leave anytime they wish. They can leave and often will until you step up your game. There are no accidents in this universe. There are only choices. Make good ones!

Write The Future Instead Of Hoping For It

If you fail to plan, you are planning to fail. I am shocked at the number of entrepreneurs, direct salespeople, small business owners, and the like who have no plan for the future. Their goal is to simply get up and try again every single day. Your plan is what keeps you going in the right direction and knowing whether or not the direction, as well as your results, are worthwhile. When you are writing the future, you are looking forward, backward, and at the present moment, all at the same time. We look forward to seeing where we wish to be at a given point in time. We look backward from that future point to determine what needs to happen in order to achieve the vision. Finally, we look at the present moment at some future point in time in order to create a vision our minds will accept. Your subconscious mind thinks in images, not words. Having a clear and concisely written vision statement, as well as clear goals, is very important. What is even more important is being able to see the reality of your success as if it is already a reality. Man never becomes that which he wants to be. He only becomes that which is accepts that he already is.

I AM! Write out your I Am statements in present tense. When you indicate what you hope to be or want to be, you are indicating lack in your life. When you write out who you are, you are accepting your future greatness now. When you do this, your subconscious begins to work diligently to discover ways of making your internal reality into an external reality. Whatever is true for you in your subconscious becomes true for you in your conscious awareness. Do not underestimate the power of being consciously aware of your future greatness now. Write the future you as present tense you, and then live as if. You've got this!

Be A Relentless Goal-Digger When It Comes To Success

I have read several times that most Americans set New Year's Resolutions. The practice of thinking about ways to make yourself better is obviously popular and definitely not new. The problem isn't whether or not people want to improve. I think people do. The problem is that 97% of people who set New Year's Resolutions will give up on them within the first 6 weeks! Only 3% of people are setting and keeping the resolutions they set at the first of the year. I have now coached hundreds of entrepreneurs and small business owners and have found most of them to simply do their best. I am all for doing our best, but I think we need a target to aim for in our pursuit of success. When we are simply trying to move forward, we lack an instrument for measuring success. Your definiteness of purpose is a critical aspect of succeeding. Each year, you have to set goals with specific measurables in order to achieve anything of true significance. Ask yourself a few key questions to get started. What do I want? When do I want it by? How will I measure it or know that I got it right? Why do I want it? What will I miss out on if I don't achieve it?

These questions help you focus your energy in a singular direction. They help you see the value in your pursuits and give you the strength to dig in when it really matters. I heard Sharon Lechter talk about the story of R.U. Darby and the story of being "3 Feet From Gold." This story is about a man who sets out to pursue his fortune in the gold mining business. He strikes an incredible vein of gold and quickly secures the necessary equipment to bring it to the surface. He gets loans from friends and family, buys the equipment, and starts working. The gold is incredible, but very short-lived. The vein soon just disappears. He digs further in but turns up empty. In frustration and desperation, he sells off the mine and the equipment to a junk man and heads home in shame. The junk man hires an expert in mining to take a look at the mine. He discovers that because of a shift in the ground years and years ago, the gold should be located 3 feet sideways from where Darby stopped digging. He kept going forward instead of sideways. The junk man dug in the direction he was advised and discovered the richest vein of gold in

California history, only 3 feet from where Darby gave up. Darby found out about what happened and vowed he would never give up on a goal again. In the insurance business, he worked diligently and pursued his objectives as a relentless goal-digger. He refused to give up on sales because of that haunting memory of what he lost when he gave up on his goals in the past. Darby struck it rich in sales, even though he had given up on the original gold/goal-mine he had discovered.

Our goals are this way as well. We go through life thinking we are nowhere near our objectives. Most of us, however, are only 3 feet from the goal-mine of our dreams. We are supposed to face struggles. That is what builds our stamina for success and prepares us to face the next challenge headed our way. The one common denominator between all great successes is, they face incredible struggles. Keep your eyes on the prize, your emotions strong, your willpower unbreakable, and your actions directed. Do this and never give up on achieving the life you have envisioned. You are only a few successes away from the life of your dreams. And then, once you are at the top, create a new mountain to climb, new goals to accomplish, new dreams to fulfill. It is your journey of achievement that shapes you into what this world truly needs!

Know What To Give Your Emotional Energy To And What Not To Care About

We give way too much attention to the things that do not matter in our lives. We worry what people think of us, what our reputation will be, whether or not our mess up is going to be permanent and so on. We focus on the one little failure we had and forget the hundreds or thousands of successes. We dwell on the bad and overlook the good. We do this because we have been conditioned our entire lives to see the shortcomings in ourselves instead of the strengths. A person will make a 98 on a paper and be angry about the 1 question out of 50 they did not answer correctly. The demon of self-doubt is an evil trickster designed to shift your focus away from your greatness and toward your lack. Here is the challenge with all of this. What you focus on will expand, always! Your mental energy needs to be tuned in to the frequency of abundance and success and victory.

Each of us should care deeply about the things that truly matter in life, the things of permanency and true significance. There just aren't very many of those things to worry about. Think about what you will look back on in your life and be the proudest of. Think about the things you will regret the most. If you are like most people, the regrets involve the things you did not do rather than the things you did do. You will regret NOT taking the risk that might have led to you being the greatest author, rock star, athlete, inventor, or whatever else you have dreamed about. Embrace your dreams! They are the visions of your potential given to you by the universe. If you waltz through life afraid to attempt your greatness, you will end your life with true regrets. If you fail the hard class, lose the bid, don't make the team, or your book never sells, who gives a shit! You will not regret the attempts at greatness. You will only regret the moments you shrank in fear of greatness. Care about the things that truly matter. Let go of the other 99% of stuff.

Get The Right Buzz Of Success Flowing Through Your Veins

Every morning wake up and say the things you are grateful for. Nothing creates a success buzz more than being grateful for the things you have in your life. I remember trying to help an acquaintance out, trying to get him to see the possibilities of life. I just wanted him to dream a little. After spending a great deal of time telling him about the good things in life, he finally decided to go look at purchasing a piece of property. That same day, he got a notice from the IRS that he had underpaid on his taxes the previous year and would owe another thousand dollars, which included penalties. He picked up the phone, called me, and cussed me out for a good five minutes. At the end of the tongue lashing he believed he was inflicting for daring to get him to see possibilities in such a crappy world, I asked him what he was grateful for. He replied that there was nothing to be grateful for and then hung up on me. That same guy has lost all of the beautiful things in his life that he did have since then. He did not appreciate having his wife and kids around. He did not appreciate his job. He did not appreciate his home. He did not appreciate any of it. His negative vibration brought negative outcomes.

Another acquaintance of mine dared to dream big dreams. He woke every day to demonstrate gratitude for the house he was renting, the wife he did not yet have, the job that was on its way, and the family he would have at some point. He was thankful for the old beater he drove because it took him to the job that would someday propel him to a great career. He practiced this gratitude every single day for years. Each year he improved his situation and moved closer to that incredible vision. Fast forward ten years from his starting point and he had a beautiful wife, a son, a home that he owned, a great pickup, a leadership role in a great company, and plenty of money. Fast forward another five years from that point and he owned a business, had two kids, a fantastic net worth, and incredible peace of mind. The difference maker was not the situational starting point or the opportunities that existed in the world. The difference maker was gratitude.

I would encourage you to say the following whenever you get the chance, and then fill in the rest of the things you are grateful for as well. Today, I am grateful for another opportunity to spin around the sun. I am grateful for the air in my lungs. I am grateful for the sun in the sky during the day and the stars and moon at night. I am thanking for another chance to chase my dreams and live a great life. I am thankful for the people in my life, all of them. I am thankful for the challenging ones for they prompt me to grow. I am thankful for the supportive ones for they comfort me in my times of need. I am thankful for the things that go wrong so that I can learn new skills. I am thankful for the things that go right so that I can advance my life forward. In all things, I am thankful and grateful!

Now, list the rest of the things in your life you have to be grateful for. Do this out loud and do it now. Do it every morning to get your day started! Once you have done that, lean into your day and do your very best to stay in the attitude of gratitude regardless of the circumstances of your day. At the end of your day, spend a few minutes listing out the things that were victories. What were your wins? What did you learn? How did you grow? IF you will be grateful in the morning and victorious at night, you will position your psyche for success and accelerate the good things you notice in your life. This accelerated success is exactly what will set you apart from everyone else around you!

Own Your Shit And Never Blame Anyone

I am so not kidding on this one! You are in charge of you, and only you can change you. There isn't anyone or anything or any group or any cosmic twist of fate to wait on. Until you step up and stop blaming anyone or anything else for where you are, you will never get to where you could be. "I'm so upset because people won't buy my services. It is such an advanced concept that people just can't get it." I heard this from a consultant starting out, and I wanted to throw up in my mouth a bit. Bullshit! That is what their whining was, just bullshit. If the concept is advanced, it was because they were not smart enough to explain it. If nobody was buying it, it was because they were not doing what was necessary to become successful. It isn't anyone else's fault. You are in charge of you. You are who you are and where you are because of the series of choices you have made in your life. Just like everyone else in this world, you have to make new choices if you want to be in a new place. If you want a new space to occupy in this life, change your concept of yourself, create a burning desire for a specific definition of life, take deliberate and focused action, be relentless in pursuing that end game, surround yourself with people who support your dreams, and get rid of the people who suck the life out of you. Do this and do it now.

One of the toughest things for us to do is to eliminate time with those who bring us down, try to steal our energy, and/or take but do not give in the relationship. I call them energy vampires because they are continuously sucking the life out of us without much, if any, contribution towards our success. They are the whiners that can't figure out why the world simply won't work right. I don't care what kind of business you are in, step up, own your shit, and take massive action right now toward your success. This is not the responsibility of anyone else. If you are in direct sales, or multi-level marketing, drop the excuses, recruit people, train people, call them every freakin' day, talk to everyone about what you believe in. Do this and do it now and don't stop until you are at the top. If you own your own business, dive head first into the business, invest time and energy and love into the endeavor. Perform the behaviors that top people perform in order to succeed. If the top performers make 50 phone calls a day, do it! If the top performers do lunch and learns, do them! Stop waiting for someone to rescue you. This is grown up land, and you are a grown up. You are the only you that exists and the only you responsible for your fate. DO NOT BLAME ANYONE FOR WHERE YOU ARE IN LIFE! I don't care where you are starting. The only thing that matters is what you choose to do next. When you fully accept responsibility for all of who you are, you can and will accomplish anything you desire.

You have to own your good and your bad, your gifts and your flaws, your mind, your body, and your soul. You have to love everyone in order to finally love yourself. You have to give up hate and jealousy and envy and anger. You have to replace all of this with a desire to see good in everyone and everything around you. You have to be in charge of every cell in your body and keep it vibrating at a frequency of love and success. This is only accomplished when you have that same positive desire for every person you encounter. What you want for another, you want for yourself. When you give up the desire for others to fail, you gain the right vibration of success. My desire is for anyone who comes in contact with this book to increase in their success, even if they don't like something about it.

Even those who do not want success, but would rather have their excuses and whining, I still desire greatness for them. I desire that they find their path to victory and embrace their ownership of their life so that we can be connected in this journey. What do you desire for you? You have to desire that for every single person on this planet in order to truly desire it for yourself. We are all connected. What you want for another, you want for yourself.

Say this out loud… I am responsible for me. I am responsible for the circumstances of life that I create from this point forward. No longer will I blame anyone or anything else for who I am or where I am. I am the person who controls my destiny, and I will take massive, deliberate, focused action toward my vision every single day. I am who I am and where I am because of my choices. I am choosing greatness today! I AM!

Thank you!

Thank you for the chance to share my thoughts with you on success. Thank you for reading this book. Thank you for striving to live your best life. Thank you for the connection we now share. I thank you because this is my vision for my life, to write and share inspiration with those who desire to move forward in life. I would encourage you to buy copies of this book for your friends, your downline, your employees, your entrepreneurial friends, or for anyone who wishes to own their place in this life. I have had an incredible time writing this book. It has challenged me, shaped me, and given me the chance to face my own shit. I would love to hear your stories about success! You can email smartassforyourbs@gmail.com to share how the book is helping you get past your shit, build a better life, and live fully into your potential. I can't wait to hear from you! You've got this!!!!!!!

Works Cited

Allen, J. (1912). *As A Man Thinketh.* Public Domain.

Csikszentmihalyi, M. (2008). *Flow.* New York: Harper Perennial Modern Classics.

DiSalvo, D. (2012, December 31). Retrieved from Psychology Today: https://www.psychologytoday.com/us/blog/neuronarrative/201212/10-reasons-why-some-people-love-what-they-do

Dowden PhD, C. (2014, June 09). *Psychology Today.* Retrieved from https://www.psychologytoday.com/us/blog/the-leaders-code/201406/why-you-should-believe-in-luck

Gallup. (2013, October 8). *News from Gallup.* Retrieved from https://news.gallup.com/poll/165269/world wide-employees-engaged-work.aspx

Hill, N. (2011). *Outwitting The Devil.* New York City: Sterling Publishing Company.

Holland, J. (2015). *My Judo Life.* Amarillo: Holland.

Lubbock, S. J. (n.d.). *The Beauties of Nature and the Wonders.*

McLeod, S. (2018). *Simply Psychology.* Retrieved from https://www.simplypsychology.org/cognitive-dissonance.html

Merchant, N. (2011, March 22). *Harvard Business Review.* Retrieved from https://hbr.org/2011/03/culture-trumps-strategy-every

O'Donnell, J. (2015, April 28). *LogMeIn.* Retrieved from Bold Chat by LogMeIn: https://blog.logmein.com/customerengagement/infographic-contact-centers-missing-mark-customer-care

Pressfield, S. (2012). *The War of Art.* Pressfield.

Robbins, M. (2017). *The 5 Second Rule.* Savio Republic.

Wattles, W. D. (1910). *The Science of Getting Rich.* Public Domain.

Wikipedia. (n.d.). Retrieved from Wikipedia: https://en.wikipedia.org/wiki/Tim_Berners-Lee

Wikipedia. (n.d.). *Wikipedia.* Retrieved from https://en.wikiquote.org/wiki/Fight_Club_(film)

Wintle, W. D. (1905). *Wikipedia.* (U. College, Producer, & Unity, 1905 edition, by Unity Tract Society, Unity School of Christianity) Retrieved September 2018, from https://en.wikipedia.org/wiki/Thinking_(poem)

ABOUT THE AUTHOR

Jody Holland is an author, speaker, executive coach, and trainer. He has a B.A. in Communications and a M.S. in Applied Psychology. He has developed dozens of training programs, coached hundreds of top executives, entrepreneurs and CEOs, been the keynote speaker at conferences more than 300 times, and trained hundreds of thousands of leaders. This is Jody's 19th published book, all of which can be found on Amazon. His author page is at: http://www.amazon.com/author/jodyholland and his website is http://www.jodyholland.com. You can find his online programs by going to his main website, or by going to www.psycheofsuccess.com.

If you are interested in having Jody speak at your next conference or event, please reach out to him through his main website. He will help your teams to reshape their thoughts, find their greatness, generate motivation, and achieve their greatest potential. He has devoted his life to helping others achieve greatness. He would love to help you and your team do the same! Please reach out through his main website at http://www.jodyholland.com.

A Few Other Books by Jody Holland

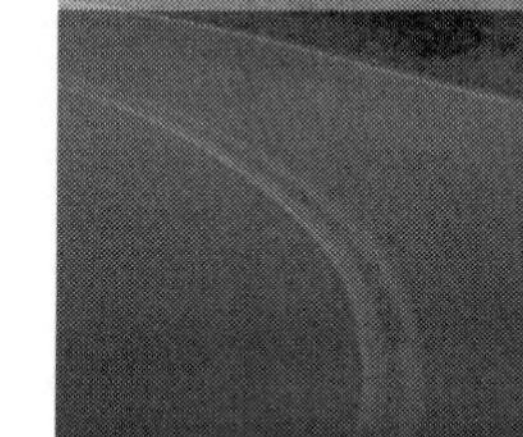

Now What!?
Yay! I'm A Supervisor!
Jody Holland

SELLING
WITH HONOR
JODY HOLLAND

HYPNOTIC
SELLING
BYPASS THE CONSCIOUS MIND
AND DISCOVER WHAT REALLY
MOTIVATES YOUR CUSTOMERS
JODY
HOLLAND

A Life of
Miracles
Jody Holland
Beginning Your
60-day Journey

Made in the USA
Columbia, SC
27 June 2023